Backstage Chronicles

BACKSTAGE CHRONICLES

Compiled by Carl Miller

ISBN 9781739663025
Copyright 2025 Astral Horizon Press
Astralhorizon.co.uk

Contributors

ACM Andy Cowan-Martin
Music impresario and manager

AG Alvin Gibbs
Bass player, UK Subs, Iggy Pop

CK Charles Kennedy
Musician, record label

CM Carl Miller
Road manager, Cat Stevens

IH Ian Hill
Bass player, Judas Priest

JM Jock McClain
Road manager, Carole King

NRS Nigel Ross-Scott
Bass player, Re-Flex

RR Rob Reynolds
Singer-songwriter

SC Sam Card
Roadie, Primal Scream and others

Contents

Alex Miller would like to thank

Thanks to everybody I have ever shared music and good vibes with; and to my beautiful miracle Bindu and our two amazing kids Luca and Nina. I am so proud of you. I love you more than yesterday.

Carl Miller would like to thank

Charles Kennedy and Astral Horizon Press for making this happen. Alex Miller for writing it. Jock McLean, Ian Hill, Alvin Gibbs, Sam Card, for their contributions. Special mention in dispatches for Dick Bell, Daisy Evans, Val & Alun Davies, Geraint Roberts, Charlie Grima, Jean Hill, Larry Steele, Alan Warner, Steve Bingham, Jerry Conway, Jean Rouselle, Chuck & Diane Conrad, Bruce & Sue Lynch, Anna Peacock, Ted Cammon, Barry Krost, and all the artists, agents, promoters, staff and crew we toured and worked with (they know who they are) that made things possible. Also, thanks to daughter Anya, daughter in law Bindu and grand offsprings Charlie, Luka, Nina and twinnies Angel and Amie for pestering me to get things finished.

Charles Kennedy would like to thank

Bandmates of years past and present – Andrew Henson, James Dawson, Louis Barfe, Steve Thorpe, Bill Wadmans, Astrid Plane. Epsom legends Catherine Bransgrove, Timothy Nathan, Jon Shepherd, Karolina Krasuska, Nancy Bear McCrea. Lucy Rob Alice and Edward Crossing. The Astral Horizon Press family – Steve Finnigan, Tegan Rielly, Bhavna Vadher, Mathew Butler, the girls and boys at Gardners Books and the London Book Fair. Working on this book has reminded me how lucky I was to find the group of friends who shared these experiences. Here's to the old days, and here's to the future.

In memory of

Andy Cowan-Martin (aka) Heyland Cowan Martin. Passed away December 2020. Greatly missed by all that knew him, and not forgotten. Knowing Andy, wherever he's gone, we bet he's found a pub open. An inspiration to all. He battled physical disabilities and health problems all his life. He could always pass a joke; a brilliant raconteur and a great friend. RIP a legend.

The Foundations: checkpoint relief

The Foundations were a seven-piece soul band that enjoyed success with hit records including Build Me Up Buttercup and many more. I'm sure it doesn't come as too much of a surprise to discover that a late 1960's soul outfit used to smoke a whole lot of dope. They really were a crazy funny bunch. As well as being stoned all the time, they used to keep me constantly busy with their antics.

On one occasion we were gigging in Germany. In those days Germany was split in two – the capitalist West (FRG) and the communist East (GDR) – so every time you crossed over from one to the other, you had to pass through West and East German checkpoints.

On one particular tour, we were heading East. Passing through yet another checkpoint – we called all checkpoints Charlies, after the famous crossing in Berlin – it was prudent not to go fucking about, as the border guards didn't have a sense of humour apart from the ones on the ground, the iffy ones were the trigger-happy buggers in the watchtowers.

The band had this big American Pontiac car that they would use to cruise around Europe. A bloody loud gold colour it was.

We arrived at the border post. I was up first for the equipment check and to clear a path for the band, as was my job. It was up to me to schmooze the guards, before waving the guys up to the guard post so they could show their passports.

I can't remember who was driving, but they touched on the gas and cruised the few hundred yards or so forward, level with the checkpoint. They slid down the windows.

All was not well.

As I mentioned, the band were big spliffers, smoked a whole lot of dope. The problem was that the checkpoint guards simply couldn't see anyone in the car through the dense clouds of marijuana smoke billowing out. Needless to say, this was not a good situation to be in, especially with East German guards everywhere, tooled up with AK-47s. I could feel the blood drain from my face. We're done for, I thought. We're all for the bloody gulag, you twats!

Finally, the smoke cleared enough so the guards could kind of see inside the car. The guards see this set of stoned black and white faces staring out at them. "Wa' happnin', man?" they asked.

The guards were not impressed, to say the least.

In a nervous kind of gibberish, I managed to explain that they were all mad musos, were mentally not well and were no threat to the communist state. I duly bribed the guards with a carton of Marlboro cigarettes, a couple the band's singles and a bunch of porno magazines (which were verboten in East Germany), in the hope they'd give us a break and let us pass.

They loved their porn, luckily. Thank God they took the bribe and waved us through. I guess they figured it wasn't worth arresting a few nutters.

Of course The Foundations being The Foundations, they didn't see anything untoward. They just drove off with more smoke and soul music blasting out of the car, completely oblivious to the fact we could have been sent off for ten years of hard labour or created an international incident. I was a dithering wreck and didn't recover until we got to Berlin and smoked a joint.

Years later, guitarist Alan Warner (the only sensible one in the band) and I were talking about the nonsense we used to get up to. He believes that day was even more farcical. He told me he had been caught viciously short in no man's land by the call of nature. He had to get out of the motor to find somewhere to go and was bricking himself (in more ways than one) in case he got arrested – you were not allowed to get out of the vehicle. He managed to find a shed in and among the barbed wire and tank traps, where he relieved himself.

I asked Alan if he'd completed his toiletries using a copy of the Soviet newspaper Pravda.

He said: "No, it was too sharp. It must have been Stalin's memoirs."

We concluded that he was maybe the only British guitarist to have left a calling card in no man's land.   **CM**

The Foundations: field of dreams

I met a chap who was jobbing at the booking agent that The Foundations used. He went by the name of Dicky Bell.

Dick became a lifelong friend of mine. Iron Maiden fans may recognise his name, as he was Maiden's long-serving production manager.

Dick was fascinated with the stories I told him about the goings on with the bands. He began pestering me to give him a job. He really wanted to get into the music business. In the end I gave in and he started with us. Things went well and we had some hilarious adventures.

Unfortunately, Dick couldn't drive at the time, so I started to teach him. On one particular occasion we happened to be doing a gig in a marquee bang in the middle of a field. While hanging around waiting for things to happen, Dick said he'd like to have a practice.

"OK," I said, thinking that he couldn't do any damage in the middle of a field.

So off he went and was doing fine in our long-wheeled base van. I turned to him: "That was cool, mate. Now try reversing."

So he crunched the gears into reverse. Bang!

"What the fuck was that?" I yelled.

We got out and discovered he had managed to reverse into a telegraph pole – the only bloody pole in the entire field.

Needless to say our wheels weren't looking so cool any more.

CM

The Foundations: high-speed dentures

While gigs certainly posed challenging moments, so could the journeys.

The ride to one particular Foundations gig in Birmingham really saw us come unstuck. We liked gigging in Brum and I knew the place well. On this particular occasion, Dicky Bell, the band's roadie at the time, had arranged a date with one of the ladies from the club and he couldn't wait to get there.

As we cruised along the motorway, a car suddenly pulled out in front of us. I slammed on the anchors big time, causing Dick to spill a joint he was rolling. This really pissed Dick off. "Pass him, Charlie, pass him," he screeched at me. I did what I was told and just as I came alongside the offending motor, Dick stuck his head out of the window. Instead of the expected vile profanity erupting from his mouth, Dick pulls his head back in: "Parl, Parl, pop the puckin' potor."

I looked at him, confused. "I can't, you prat, I'm doing 70 miles an hour. Why?"

With a strange look on his face he began to reply. "My pucking peeth have pallen out."

"Your teeth have fallen out?" I was truly astonished. I couldn't believe what had happened. It never occurred to me that he had false teeth.

Eventually we pulled over. Dick insisted we had to go back and find them.

Trying really hard not to laugh, I pointed out that it would be of no use as they dropped out at least a couple of miles back and had probably been squashed under the wheels of a truck by now. Reluctantly, he accepted the inevitable and we cracked on to the gig.

While I was setting up the sound system, a couple of the guys asked me what was up with Dick, as he was not talking to anyone. I told them the story and they all fell about in stitches of laughter.

Of course, from that moment on they wound him up rotten. "Where's your date, man?" they asked, trying to make him laugh.

Poor old Dick never left backstage that night and he never got to meet his date, but his story helped make him a legend in the business.
                                                                    CM

Stevie Wonder drives

One memorable highlight of touring with The Foundations was going on a UK package tour with Stevie Wonder.

It was 1969. The Foundations were the middle act and opening the show was the female group The Flirtations. We played the Odeon and theatre circuit and all the acts travelled on the same bus, so that was real hoot. There was always a party atmosphere on the bus and Stevie was always in the thick of it. He was known for his sense of fun.

On one particular day, everyone boarded the bus and the usual banter started while waiting for Stevie to get on. A few minutes later, he was guided onto the bus, engine ticking over.

He climbed aboard, but instead of going to his normal seat, found his way to the driver's seat and started to rev the engine. The girls start screaming and freaking out, thinking he was going to drive. Of course Stevie thought winding everyone up was really fun.

CM

The Foundations in the Deep South

Touring the southern states of the US in the 1960s was a pain in the arse for many reasons.

I remember going into this diner one night with The Foundations – a mixed colour band, of course. Not only were we all different colours, we had long hair and really flamboyant outfits. So we walked into this place in Georgia and sat down, as you do in American diners. You sit round in a square – an island, as they call them. We started looking at the menu to see what was on offer.

The next thing we knew, at this neighbouring island was a bunch of redneck truck drivers. It wasn't long before they piped up.

"You guys or chicks?" they began baiting us.

So I was thinking: Oh no, this ain't going to be pretty.

"God dammit, you got n*****s. You got n*****s and you got f*****s!" they started taunting.

I feared this was going to get really hairy.

The atmosphere became more and more strained. The torrent of abuse continued for a while, before it really got too much. Next thing you know, our bus driver couldn't take any more and he just snapped. He stood up, picked up a stool and threw it at them. The next thing you knew, it was like a Wild West saloon. Fighting broke out, stools were flying everywhere, food was hurled across the room, fists started flying and blood started getting spilled.

The funny thing was that it soon became obvious to us that none of this mindless violence was coming our way. Crazily, the truckers had all started fighting with each other. God knows why, but needless to say we didn't stop to find out and skulked out of there. We just let the idiots get on with it. You could still hear the rumble continuing as we got back on our bus and drove the hell out of there.   **CM**

The Foundations' van plan breaks down

We waved goodbye to our cool wheels when The Foundations' accountant, Michael Levy – now Lord Levy and a long-standing pal of Tony Blair, advised the guys that, for tax purposes, it was better to rent a van. So Dick and I picked up a rental van from Avis. While it wasn't cool, it was at least brand new. We set off for Northern Ireland to play Belfast, where the band had a great reception and got a bit out of it afterwards.

As a result, the next day we were late setting off for Dublin. Complete with hangovers, we finally managed to get going. We arrived at the border checkpoint – in those days there was a hard border between the North and the Republic – and were relieved that we seemed to have picked up some time.

Speeding ahead, we found ourselves travelling on a series of B roads. We shot round a bend only to come upon a tractor that had broken down, blocking the road. Alongside the farmer was a member of the local Garda (police) looking on.

There was no way I was going to stop in time. I took the only other route open to me and crashed through a hedge into a field full of cows.

Fortunately, apart from a dented front and wings, the van stayed upright and we and the cows survived unhurt. I managed to slide the van back out onto the road.

We told the cop who we were and slipped him a copy of the band's single. He was amused more than anything: "You'll be English then. That explains it all." And off we went.

As we entered Dublin, the van was definitely not well. There was steam coming from the engine and the wheels seemed a little wobbly. We went through an intersection to cross a bridge. Bang! A car smacked straight into the side of us. We got out and surveyed the damage, then swapped particulars with the other driver. As we did so, we noticed a signpost at the side of the bridge: Ballsbridge. You could say that again!

Eventually we turned up at the gig, just in time to save the show. We were met by Eric, the trombonist. "Rassa man, where you bin?"

We told him about the crashes.

He calmly replied. "Is the gear OK, man?"

"Yeah," we muttered.

"Oh man! That's OK then," said Eric and wandered off.

Dick and I exchanged a look.

We managed to limp the van onto the ferry and, with plenty of nursing, got it back to the Avis depot in London. I tore into the Reception area, pretending I was in a rush, and dropped the keys on the desk. "I've bought your van back. Here are the keys. I've got to dash. Oh, by the way, we had a bit of a bump. It's not too bad. Bye."

Before the receptionist could get a word in, I had already scarpered.

I'm not sure what Levy thought after sorting out the insurance claims for the repairs. I thought it best not to ask.   **CM**

The Average White Band: sleeping like a log

The Foundations had a regular gig in Stockholm at Alexandra's Club, a swanky upmarket joint at the time. The girls were stunning and the drugs were plentiful. We would gig there for a week at a time. As a part of the deal, we were given the use of the flat above the club, where we could hang and crash out.

We always used to bump into other bands coming or going, doing the same circuit. It was here that I first bumped into a great band called the Dream Police, an R&B band from Glasgow. They were a really hard-nosed party band and later went on to become well-known as the Average White Band.

One night, one of the guys in the band – I don't remember who exactly – got so fucked up that he ended up crashed out on one of the beds. He wasn't just fucked up… he was really fucked up. He was supposed to be up the next morning but ended up oversleeping by two bloody days! During this time, nobody could get him up, despite us trying everything we could think of: music, noise, water, you name it.

He was so out of it that one of the guys, in his infinite wisdom, decided to play a prank on him. They peeled the sheets back off his bed while he was still out of it and placed some unmentionable natural products in the bed with him. He lay there for a few more hours with the 'waste' in his bed. When he finally woke up he went completely crazy – let's just say that he didn't see the funny side of it. Of course nobody owned up to the prank.

CM

Ginger Baker and the curse

When The Foundations disbanded in 1970, I found myself looking for another gig. But where should I go? These sorts of jobs weren't advertised. It was all word of mouth or through somebody you knew. I had landed The Foundations gig due to a Brummie pal of mine, Roy Lemon, The Move's roadie, recommending me.

The best place to look for work was where the bands and roadies hung out. The three London hangouts that were happening in those days were The Speakeasy, The Marquee and The Ship pub on Wardour Street in Soho. I picked a night I knew would be heaving and trotted off to The Marquee, stopping in at The Ship on the way.

When I arrived at The Marquee, I knew it was going to be a good night because of the number of band vans that were parked out on the street, plus the general whiff of weed that hung in the air. I strolled in without paying because I knew Jack the manager, and squeezed my way through the joint smoke and to the bar, bumping into some familiar faces along the way. The guys from The Small Faces were in, The Nice were in, along with a further assortment of half-blitzed musos and roadies. There was usual banter – "Hey man, how ya doin?" – coupled with trendy American handshakes.

"Yeah man, I'm cool. I'm looking for a gig now The Foundations have busted up. Know anything going?" I casually asked a number of faces.

"Try Little Ginger. I heard he was looking for a mate," a stoned roadie with a Jack Daniels in his hand informed me. Little Ginger, aka Colin Smythe, was Cream's roadie.

Colin was a definitive cheeky cockney. He was nicknamed Little Ginger because of his red hair and being somewhat smaller than Ginger Baker, Cream's drummer, who was actually quite tall and skinny.

I eventually found Little Ginger. I knew of him by reputation, but we had never met. Fortunately he had heard of me too. In those days, if you worked with a hit band you became a member of the inner circle, which was actually fairly small. We hit it off straight away and I was on board.

Colin explained to me that as Cream had also split, Ginger Baker had formed a new big band called Ginger Baker's Air Force with an all-star line-up, which included the likes of Steve Winwood. Colin had been seconded for some UK and European gigs. He explained the ins and outs of it all and added that it might be a bumpy ride because the dates were all over the place and Ginger Baker was having big drug problems. I had heard the talk and was not surprised. It was one druggy band.

So off we set off in our 3-ton truck. Little Ginge was right. The tour was all over the frigging place. It looked like someone had thrown darts into a map. Up and down the country like a yo-yo. Then the inevitable occurred when Ginger Baker pulled a no-show.

The bummer was that Little Ginge had received a tip off from the agents, but we had to go ahead and make the set-up look as normal as possible. When the promoter finally found out, he gave Little Ginge and I a huge bollocking. And when he announced to the audience that the show was cancelled, all hell broke loose. We were the unfortunate ones who had to strike the stage amid the booing and cursing, dodging bottles and all kinds of missiles as we went about our work packing away the gear.

Of course Little Ginge, in his cryptic cockney way, would always come up with a remark. "Fucking great to be loved, eh Charlie? They could have fucking chucked a bottle with something in it," he joked.

"This is the fucking life, hey Col?" I replied.

On he went: "What you moaning about? You're getting paid fuck all for this."

Once the UK dates were over, we faced a long drive down to Switzerland – hard work in a 3-ton truck that only went 60mph. Downhill.

By then, our banter was well refined, making the journey easier – we could have done a stint at the London Palladium. Halfway down France, we were doing well on time, so Little Ginge suggested we pull off the road and find a bed and breakfast for our night stop. We pulled off and managed to find a little town. We drove around and spotted a small guest house. Little Ginge told me to park the truck and that he would go and suss it out. I stopped the truck in a large park opposite the hotel.

Ginge returned. "We're in mate. It's a bit on the JR side," meaning 'rank', Cockney rhyming slang for very iffy or something rude. It was taken from J Arthur Rank, the film producer.

The room was OK. Two beds and a basin. It was certainly better than sleeping in the truck. Sheer joy. We crashed out, only to be rudely awoken at six in the morning by a loud knock on our door. "Police! Police! Police! Se lever! Get up, get up!"

Freaked out, we sprang out of bed. We thought we were being busted. We opened the door to the gendarmerie and they waved us out frantically. They didn't speak any English, but we followed them out of the main door, where they started pointing to the truck and pointing back at us. "Le camion. The truck," they said, seeming to be very pissed off.

"Oui, yeah," we replied. I looked over and it turned out that I had inadvertently parked the bloody thing in the middle of a market square. Overnight, the weekly market had sprung up around it. The truck was now in a sea of market stalls. What a balls up!

After a lot of shrugging of shoulders and muttering under their breath, we were frog-marched to the truck by the police and told to move it. Easier said than done. The police forced the traders to take down the stalls in front of us in order to clear a path. That really pissed them off, understandably. It was the best part of an hour before we finally managed to drive clear, but not before we upset a couple of stalls and crushed a load of fruit and vegetables.

We received a severe verbal lashing. Luckily we didn't understand most of it. But I had never seen so many pissed off French people before. Entente Cordiale or not, Anglo-French relations hit an all-time low.

We finally got trucking again. During the drive, we got talking about what a strange bunch this band was. We agreed it was not a happy group. "Man, it's down to the drugs," Little Ginge said, laughing. "They're all off their fucking heads."

They were the only band I ever worked with that I never got to know. None of them.

We arrived in Switzerland for the Montreux Jazz Festival on Lake Geneva. We soon discovered that Ginger hadn't made it and that we should hang around for more news. The next day, Little Ginge informed me that Ginger had finally arrived, but had got pulled by Swiss customs for you know what. It was time for us to check out.

Just as Little Ginge and I were leaving, we bumped into Graham Bond, the band's keyboard player. He was at the hotel reception having a huge argument over his bill. Graham was well known for doing drugs. He was also into witchcraft and was a big follower of the occultist Aleister Crowley. The row intensified and Graham started chanting maniacally and waving his arms about. He was putting curses on the hotel and staff.

Colin and I looked at each other with amazement. "Let's blow, man, before he turns us into fucking planks."

A few years later, Graham Bond had come to a very grisly finish under a tube train at Finsbury Park station. He was in poor mental health – by that time he thought he was Crowley's son. Perhaps his curse had rebounded?

After that trip, I never got to work with Little Ginge again, but we remained good pals and stayed in touch. Unfortunately, while on tour with Eric Clapton, he was tragically killed in a helicopter crash in East Troy, Wisconsin in August 1990, along with four others including guitar legend Stevie Ray Vaughan. In marginal weather, the pilot, only rated for instrument flight in fixed wing aircraft, flew into a man-made ski hill that was printed on the chart but obscured by fog.

"Well, a chopper was a bit flashier than a 3-ton truck, hey Charlie?" I could imagine Little Ginge saying.   **CM**

The Sweet's crazy house

Around 1969, while working with The Foundations, I found myself looking for a new pad.

I can't remember how it came to pass, but I moved into a semi-detached house on Cleveland Gardens in Hendon, a leafy North London suburb, with a chap called Mick Stewart. Mick was a right Jack the lad. He had been the guitarist in Johnny Kidd & the Pirates, a well-known band at the time.

I didn't know it at the start, but this place was to become a real loony bin. I ended up living there until mid-1972. During that time, all types of musos and people in the music game came and went. Mick joined glam metal band The Sweet, who went on to rival Slade with a string of major hits. Members of The Sweet and The Foundations came and went and the place became a groovy place for wild parties.

During this period, I joined Cat Stevens and so another collection of band members started to swing by. Cat Stevens' drummer Gerry Conway moved in. He had previously played and knocked around with members of Fairport Convention, so he brought with him a folk-based crowd.

The place was jumping virtually 24-7 and what a gas it was. The parties were insane and never seemed to stop. Some of the most amazing impromptu jam sessions kicked off in there. Guys from The Sweet would have a blow with Cat's band. Members of Fairport Convention would jam with a collection of jumbled up stars. Someone would start strumming and it would kick off from there. Instruments were always lying around and I always kept a load of equipment in the garage, so there was never a lack of gear.

We were all constantly coming or going to one place or another, but whoever was at the house never needed an excuse for a bash. It would be quite normal to arrive back from a gig at two or three in the morning and find a party in full swing. We would simply join in.

It was during the summer months that it really used to take off. You would always find someone crashed out on the landing or out of it lying in the garden. There were always various items of male and female clothing hanging off something or lurking in strange places. Mysteriously, the items never seemed to belong to anyone and nobody would ever claim ownership.

Another puzzling thing was a never-ending supply of joints and booze that seemed to magically self-perpetuate. Amazingly, the place never got raided and I don't even recall any of the neighbours complaining.

Perhaps they enjoyed the parties too.   **CM**

How I met Cat Stevens

You may be interested to know how it came to pass that I got to work with Cat Stevens.

The Foundations had split. I had the odd tour of Europe with Uriah Heep and Ginger Baker's Air Force and some other one-nighters, such as mixing sound for The Old Time Music Hall.

The Music Hall was a great experience. You could at least have a laugh with the old ladies belting out My Old Man Said Follow The Van. But I was sick of jumping from one band to another and wanted a long-term gig similar to the one I had with The Foundations. When you work with an act for a while, you become part of the act. You don't get that feeling when you're freelancing. But where to start looking for a new gig?

First thing was to do some backtracking, so I popped in to see The Foundations' agent Mike Dolan, fellow Brummie and Aston Villa supporter. Mike had recently left The Foundations' organisation to have crack on his own. He went on to manage many successful acts, including The Strawbs, Judas Priest, The Tourists and Eddy Grant.

Mike mentioned that he'd heard Cat Stevens was looking for a tour manager. He had the name and number of his management company and told me to give them a call. So I rang the Barry Krost Management office and a very well-spoken secretary answered the phone. I explained the reason for the call and she put me through to Barry Krost, who spoke like a character from a Noël Coward play. He arranged a time for me to pop in and see him later that day.

I arrived at his office at 27 Curzon Street, 200 yards from The Playboy Club, while the next-door basement was an upmarket brothel. Next door on street level was The White Elephant, a club for the artistic elite. I went into the office looking as cool as I could in a very rock star way. I introduced myself to a very Chelsea looking lady with a very Chelsea sounding name: Jill St Amont. We chatted for a while until this dapper looking guy came in. He was David Evans, also known as Daisy or Dais for short. He went on to become personal assistant extraordinaire to some huge names in the biz, most notably Freddie Mercury.

"Barry can see you now," Daisy sang as he ushered me into Krost's office. The room was typical of an impresario. Plush chesterfield settees, objets d'art and plenty of the trappings associated with being a media mogul.

We started to talk. He asked me about my experience and I explained that I had toured Europe and the US many times. He seemed quite pleased. He asked me if I could go and meet Cat Stevens there and then, explaining that he would have the final say.

"Yes, of course," I replied.

He picked up the phone and rang Stevens. He told him my name and that I would come over immediately. I suspect Barry was somewhat relieved that I knew all about the "ghastly rock business", as it meant that he wouldn't have to be as involved. As I was to discover, Barry Krost's company was actually a theatrical agency and Cat Stevens was the only music act on its books at the time. All his other clients were actors, directors and so on – it would be quite normal to bump into famous film and stage stars of the day, including Peter Finch, Angela Lansbury, Get Carter director Mike Hodges and playwright John Osborne, the original angry young man. Unsurprisingly, Barry Krost would go on to enjoy a successful career as a film producer in Hollywood with films such as the Ike and Tina Turner biopic What's Love Got To Do With It?

Anyway, I made my way over to Cat Stevens' flat, which was above his parents' cafe at the end of Shaftesbury Avenue. When I arrived, he was sitting in the lotus position, caressing a black Gibson Everly Brothers guitar. Alun Davies, his guitarist, was rolling a cigarette, while Larry Steele sported the biggest Afro hair I'd ever seen – he had just joined the duo on bass. They were rehearsing with Larry to get him acquainted with the material.

We began chatting away and I discovered that everyone referred to Cat Stevens as Steve. They asked me the same questions as Barry: what had I done and who did I know? I dropped in some gossip to break the ice and asked what their plans were, how organised they were and what gear they had? They said they had some university gigs coming up. On the spot, I figured out some ideas for the tour and made suggestions. They wanted to know if I could pull them together in time for the gigs? I didn't want to look too flash or over-confident: "Erm, probably. Give me a minute or two and I'll let you know."

I shot out onto Shaftesbury Avenue, looking to find a phone box – no mobiles in 1971! I felt pretty confident about calling in some favours, as I knew my credibility was good with all the major suppliers around town. I made some connections and had the logistics of the tour virtually sewn up in a matter of three or four calls. I added in some extras for good measure.

On my return to the flat, I announced that it was all fixed and I received nods of approval. I got the gig and couldn't help thinking that this was going to be so cool. Just what the doctor ordered. It would be a blank page; I would free to set things up how I wanted, with no interference.

That was the beginning of a halcyon period for me. Within a very short time, as I had hoped, I had been given carte blanche to arrange everything to do with the music side of the business. Barry Krost didn't have to muck about in the ghastly rock 'n' roll world, except when he wanted to attend the most prestigious gigs and receptions. He always looked grandiose, bless him.

One of the best things about working with Steve, and why he was so different, was that he constantly progressed. He was very artistic, exotic, innovative and always exciting – far from your run of the mill rock 'n' roll outfits. And the theatrical atmosphere surrounding Barry Krost Management had a major influence on many Cat Stevens productions.   **CM**

Cat Stevens' morning has broken

Cat Stevens and the band were about halfway through making the Teaser And The Firecat album, which came out in October 1971. Things were going really well at the recording session at Morgan Studios in London.

When Steve was recording, I would normally sit in the control room, to be on hand to deflect any intrusions or take care of any other business or issues that cropped up. Steve was 100% focused when recording, rehearsing or while he was in work mode. He hated interruptions when he was in full flow and would really get uptight and mightily pissed off. It was a case of "Carl, you deal with it."

He'd just finished off one track and producer Paul Samwell-Smith and the engineer were setting up the desk for the next, which was going to be Morning Has Broken. I knew he was going to record the song as he'd mentioned it to me in advance. I must confess it didn't seem to me – or plenty of others at the time – that a traditional hymn would fit on the album. What did we know?

Anyway. I went through the studio to take a phone call. When I returned, Steve was at the piano, playing around with the intro, looking a little frustrated.

"What's up?" I asked.

He looked at me and groaned:"I can't quite get this bit right."

Pondering for a moment, I mentioned that I knew of someone who could do the part a treat.

"Who's that then?" he said, bemused, as if to say, what do you know about it?

"A chap called Rick Wakeman. He's classically trained, plays keyboards with The Strawbs."

"Can you get hold of him?" Steve asked.

"Sure." I jumped back on the phone, this time to Strawbs manager Mike Dolan. I put Mike in the picture, gave him all the info and he put the wheels in motion.

Rick duly turned up at the agreed time. He listened to the track and had a little tinkle. Bang. He nailed it. The rest was history, as they say.

So forget what Wikipedia and other such sources say about how Cat's version of the song was created. You've just heard it straight from the horse's mouth. **CM**

Cat Stevens: green tea for the tillerman

I believe it was Steve Winwood who recommended the benefits of drinking green tea to Cat Stevens.

Now, I'm not saying Steve was gullible, but he absorbed everything like that. If it was the latest health kick or someone told him it was good for his karma, he'd have it. He would then, at great insistence, advise everyone around him to drink the brew. Of course everybody would say, "Oh yeah, great man," then slyly pour it away somewhere.

During this fetish period for green tea he would nag me to make sure there was always a plentiful supply to hand. I did, of course, otherwise all hell would let loose. It seemed he'd focus on something like tea, rather than an issue with the equipment or something. I guess that was my problem.

We were on an early US tour and arrived in New York to play the legendary Carnegie Hall. The day was going well, and by now Steve was enjoying the witch's brew – as the crew had christened it – on a regular basis. Carnegie was totally sold out and was attended by the great and the good. The show began and Cat was off to a flying start.

During most shows I used to stand in the wings to keep an eye on proceedings. However, on this occasion, part way through the show, I was called away to deal with some issue or other. At which point, I heard Steve calling: "Carl! Where's Carl?" I thought, what the fucking hell is up now?

In a frenzy, I dashed back towards the stage, which was not easy as it was dark and there were loads of obstructions about. The next song ended. He turned and saw me., then called me out onto the stage.

Oh no, I was thinking, trying to look as cool as I could in front of a couple of thousand people and celebs in the front row. I walked over to him perched. Giving me a black look, he said: "Can I have my tea?"

I walked off, trying to look unflappable, despite feeling highly embarrassed. I organised the brew and waited in the wings until the next song ended. The audience finished applauding, so I strolled back on stage, with this bloody cup of tea in my hand – still trying to keep my cool.

I handed it over, turned and walked back. Halfway to the wings, I heard Steve say: "That was Carl, my tour manager." At which point there was a round of applause, adding to my general sense of embarrassment.

In hindsight, there can't be many tour managers that can say they've received a round of applause at Carnegie Hall. Of course I didn't live it down and for the next few days all of the guys took the piss. All I heard for a while was: "Fancy a cuppa, Charlie?"
                                                                    CM

Cat Stevens' Rolls-Royce vanishes

Most of the rock stars I've ever met have all had a 'me' moment and Cat Stevens was no exception.

One of these was when he informed me that, on arrival in San Francisco, he wanted me to arrange to have a white Rolls-Royce to pick him up and ferry him about.

No problem.

We arrived in San Fran and were met by the usual entourage of greeters and the odd fan who had found out our schedule, plus the Roller. It was a 1950s model – possibly a Silver Cloud – the type of car you would expect to see a member of the royal family emerging from in a black and white newsreel.

Steve was introduced to the necessary people and signed some autographs. I had him ushered off to his carriage while I caught up with the promoter to get an update on arrangements for the gig. After a quick chat, I made my way out to the pickup point, where Steve was waiting with the Roller – and this odd looking geezer. They were chatting away, so I didn't think any more of it.

"Mount up, let's go," I said as we jumped in the Roller.

To my surprise the geezer got in as well.

We arrived at the hotel and I checked Steve in and gave him his room key. As I put him in the elevator I asked him who the guy was, as he was still lurking about shiftily.

"He's a fan. Seems like a nice guy, so I offered him a lift into town," Steve replied.

I had never known that happen before.

I told Steve: "I've got to get over to the venue ASAP to take care of some urgent production business. I'll see you there at 3pm for the sound check."

We always tried to soundcheck at that time because, with Steve, they were always akin to a marathon.

Once at the venue, I resolved any issues and appeased the odd VIP or two with last-minute extra seat requests. At which point a call went out: I was wanted on the phone.

I walked into the production office and asked who it was. It was Steve and I was warned that he sounded really pissed off.

Shit. Now what?

I picked up the phone: "Hi mate."

Before I could get anything else out, he shouted: "WHERE'S MY FUCKING CAR, MAN? WHY HAVE YOU TAKEN MY CAR? YOU SHOULD HAVE TOLD ME."

Steve carried on venting on for a bit longer.

Finally, I was able to tell him that I hadn't got his car and that it was outside the hotel with the driver when I left.

"Well, where is it then? I'll be late!" he puffed.

"I don't know, but I'll send someone over to pick you up and I'll try and find out what happened to it," I groaned.

He got to the soundcheck in another car (and not in a great mood) and sure enough the soundcheck that day turned into a marathon.

A little later I discovered what had happened. It turned out that the odd-looking geezer had spoken to the driver of the Rolls-Royce and told him that Mr Stevens had given the OK for the driver to take him home. Of course, he stopped off at numerous places en route and, at each and every stop, he took an age. He must have visited everyone he knew, posing with Cat Stevens' Rolls-Royce. Cheeky git.

We never saw the Roller again. It's probably still driving around California for all I know.   **CM**

Cat Stevens and the last führer

One of the most bizarre things that happened to me while I was with Cat Stevens was during a tour of Europe. We were performing in Bremen and were booked in at one of the most beautiful and expensive hotels in the country, just outside the city.

On the afternoon of the show, prior to soundcheck, Steve asked me to go back to the hotel as he had forgotten something and would I retrieve it from his room. No problem.

I got back to the hotel and duly picked the forgotten item before making my way back down in the lift. Reaching the ground floor, the doors opened and there was a load of commotion in the lobby area, with people buzzing all over the place. I walked through the mêlée and was forced to squeeze past this elderly gentleman at the centre of the fuss.

On my way out, I stopped to ask the concierge what was happening He explained that the elderly man was 'The Admiral'.

"The Admiral?" I asked.

He replied: "Ja, das ist der Grand Admiral Donitz."

I was completely gobsmacked. Karl Donitz was the man designated by Adolf Hitler in his last will and testament to be his successor after he committed suicide. As such, he was the second and last führer of the Third Reich.

When I got back and told the lads, one of them asked if I had sung Two World Wars And One World Cup to him! **CM**

Cat Stevens gets his rocks off

One thing you could always rely on with Cat Stevens was a curveball coming from left field.

One such quirk came on one of our days off when we were in Japan. On all of Cat's tours, we always had at least one day off between shows so that his voice was always rested. It was an expensive luxury, as the costs of being on the road were almost the same whether you played a show or not. Many bands will do four or five shows back-to-back before a day off. Doing it our way had many benefits. Apart from taking in the sights and sounds of the local area, it allowed ample time to move the production from one venue to the next.

On this occasion we were staying at the Tokyo Hilton. Steve cornered me and told me to arrange for the two of us to go to Kyoto on our day off. He'd heard that the Ryoanji Temple Rock Garden was well worth a visit. "Of course," I said.

Bollocks, just my fucking luck. I had already made plans. Some of the lads had arranged to go to a bathhouse for a session. They reckoned there was a place where the geishas would beat customers with cherry blossom branches, followed by a scrub with a soapy lotus petal loofah.

After several hours, Steve and I arrived in Kyoto and were given a guided tour by Ishi, the tour promoter's assistant. Steve was shown the rock garden by a monk and afterwards settled down to meditate. Meanwhile, I was thinking to myself, here I am looking at bloody rocks instead of having a relaxing day off. That said, you couldn't help but appreciate the place and take in the architecture and tranquil atmosphere.

We finally arrived back in Tokyo late into the evening. Steve was in a good mood, so from that point of view, it was worth it. Having Steve calm was always a good thing. He retired to bed and I wandered into the hotel bar.

A few of the band were in there. "Hey man, how'd you get on? What did you do?"

"We looked at rocks."

"Rocks?" came the bemused reply.

"Yep. How was Tokyo Rose? Did you get a good walloping?"

"Oh man, it was great. You really missed out."

"Arigato, mate," I grumbled and downed a cocktail.

That was my day off in Japan.   **CM**

Salvador Dali on display

As an art director, I have been asked to design and create many interesting commissions. For one reason or another, I was getting loads of commissions from bands and singers to design album sleeves. On one particular occasion, I got a call from an old pal and school chum, Mike Dolan, who was managing British folk group The Strawbs at the time.

He asked:"Could you do the sleeve for their forthcoming album?"

Although a quintessential albums band, The Strawbs are, ironically, best known for their 1970s single Part Of The Union. While successful in the UK, it was across the pond in the United States that they really seemed to capture people's imagination and enjoyed a great deal of success. In their pomp, they were a very serious and arty band.

They obviously liked my work, as I was invited to join them in New York for their US tour.

Whenever they performed in New York, they always stayed at the discerning and most prestigious Saint Regis in the heart of Manhattan, one of the most luxurious hotels in the world. The five-star diamond hotel is an 18-storey French Beaux-Arts style building built by John Jacob Astor in 1904, with breathtaking attention to detail. It is situated on Fifth Avenue, four blocks from Central Park.

I was made aware that Marlene Dietrich had lived in the hotel, along with other stars and celebs of the time. However, it was the great surrealist artist Salvador Dali and his wife Gala that were in situ on a couple of occasions I stayed there. It was well known that they liked to make the place home during the winter months.

On this particular tour, the band's tour manager – good friend and fellow Brummie Carl Miller – had recently finished some Cat Stevens dates and had picked up the Strawbs tour to earn some freelance cash while Cat was having a break. One morning during our stay, Carl and I went down for breakfast. We sat down and I leaned over and whispered to him as discreetly as I could: "Do you know who that is over there?"

"No," he said, after taking a subtle glance.

I blurted in a hushed voice: "It's FUCKING Salvador Dali, you divot. World famous artist. I'm a big fan."

While residing at the hotel, Dali could often be found in the coffee shop, hosting 'look at me' sessions. These occasions saw Dali sitting inside a roped-off area as Manhattan's society ladies were charged $5 or $10 each for the privilege of doing nothing other than admiring him up close. Dali would sit inside the ropes looking resplendent, but completely motionless, his pristine moustache styled and dangling, silver knob cane in hand. He wouldn't talk to the ladies – they were only allowed to talk via his wife or simply admire him, drink coffee and depart. As one session would end, another would promptly begin and another group of ladies would be allowed access to his forum. It was surreal and really quite unbelievable to watch. It was like he was acting out an image of himself, turning his existence into a work of art.

Away from fans, photographers and the press, he was a little bit more straightforward. After a couple of mornings, we were on nodding terms. On one occasion, Dali told us he was a fan of the Strawbs, because he appreciated "the artistic flair of the group." To this day, we still don't believe he knew who we were or what we were all about. He was just being charming or perhaps letting us know he was 'with it'.

H had a wicked sense of humour and loved having the last word. You could never be quite sure when he was joking and when he was being serious. He looked like he was always happy to sign an autograph or two, followed by a jocular comment such as: "That will be $10, por favor." We were convinced he said these things to provoke some kind of reaction. A member of the hotel staff who spoke Spanish told me that, on one occasion, Dali had gone berserk, raging over an objet d'art that he described as "monstruosidad" and commanded it be thrown out and "destruida".

If we saw him about, we would always ask "How you doin?" in thick Brummie accents, which he found most peculiar. Two worlds colliding.

They say never meet your heroes, but I fondly look back to meeting one of mine.   **JM**

Cat Stevens' favourable weed exchange

One of the great things about working with Cat Stevens was that there was always something different different from the normal run of the mill rock 'n' roll stuff going on.

His management company for example was run by Barry Krost, a theatrical agent with Steve as the only music type in his stable – all his other clients were actors. He worked with the likes of Joan Collins, Richard Gere, Liza Minnelli and Matthew Perry. It would be quite normal to bump into a famous film star at the office and, fortunately for me, I got to know many of them.

It was within this alternative atmosphere that all kinds of different ideas were spawned.

Steve was a huge star at the time, having achieved enormous worldwide success with five previous albums and set to record a sixth, to be called Foreigner.

For some time we'd been talking about it and he mentioned that for this album he wanted to try something different and with a different line-up of musicians. He had been getting into sounds coming out of Chicago and Philadelphia, so I was quite prepared for a change of direction.

One day I was in Barry Krost's office and having a laugh with my good mate David 'Daisy' Evans, the office manager and

Barry's PA. Steve was in a meeting with Barry and, all of a sudden, I was called in. "Carl, we are going to start the album in a couple of weeks. We want you to organise things." That wasn't unusual.

"Where are we doing it?" I asked, expecting it to be in one of the big studios in London.

"Kingston," said Steve.

I struggled to recall a world class recording studio in Kingston-upon-Thames, a suburb of southwest London.

"No, Kingston, Jamaica! Byron Lee's studio!"

Island Records founder Chris Blackwell had a share in the studio and the likes of Bob Marley had recorded there, so they was pretty confident it would work.

Oh, wow, I thought. What a wheeze!

Barry added: "You'll all be staying at Chris's old residence, the Terra Nova." (For the uninitiated, this is the most luxurious boutique hotel in Kingston. "But first, Steve will go to the New York office to meet with Nat and sign off on the finances." Nat Weiss was his US attorney and his other clients included George Harrison and James Taylor.

Steve added: "I'll see you there. Oh and by the way, I'll need all my gear."

He didn't just mean a suitcase, of course. He meant a whole heap of shit: keyboards, guitars, amps and a whole lot more.

Bugger, I thought. I knew there'd be a catch. How was I going to get all the right customs paperwork for all that gear in time?

My idea was to take the whole lot on as personal baggage, but it was a bit much for one person. What to do?

I called Ken Berry in New York. He was the owner of Studio Instrument Rentals (SIR), which had depots all across America, specialising in every type of musical equipment you could name. I knew Ken and was confident he'd come through for me. I explained the situation to him and told him that he could take a flight to Jamaica that arrived an hour after mine. He was well up for the trip, especially after I told him we were staying at the Terra Nova and not to worry about the money! "Just bill Nat in New York," I told him. We agreed I'd wait for him at the airport.

So far so good. I checked in at Heathrow early as I had so much crap with me. I handed over my ticket to the girl on the reception desk.

"Are you checking in any bags, sir?"

"Yes, they are just coming," I replied nonchalantly. At which point two porters arrived puffing and pulling two flatbed carts.

The agent looked on in disbelief. "Is this all yours?" she gulped.

"Oh yeah, yeah," acting as if this was all normal.

"Well, I'll have to charge you excess, sir," she said rather sheepishly.

I was not at all surprised, but decided to act disappointed.

"Oh dear. I suppose you do." I feigned a sigh.

Eventually, the poor girl checked in all of the items and I ambled off, leaving a load of pissed off passengers queuing behind.

On arrival in Kingston, I was upbeat on one hand and full of trepidation on the other, wondering what kind of treatment I was going to get from the customs officers. All of the gear came off the plane and two full trolleys made it to customs. Interestingly, the desk was stationed outdoors – on account of the climate, I suppose.

A customs officer strolled over in my direction. He eyed up the gear and asked whether it was all mine. I explained that we had come to record some music with Cat Stevens at Byron Lee's studios. The officer looked at me. "I play some stuff ya know? Rass man, dat cool."

Meanwhile, a crowd of customs guys had gathered around, getting in on the action and debating what was the best band in town. Meanwhile, my guy started reggae dancing, while stamping all the gear.

When it was all stamped, I thanked the guy for his help and slipped him a drink (or two). I casually mentioned that my pal Ken was arriving soon from New York with another cartload of equipment. "Is that cool?" I asked.

"Ya man, we take care of it," he replied.

Feeling pretty smug, I waited for Ken. His plane soon arrived and, in what felt like minutes, he was stood next to me with all his gear stamped, over the moon with the efficiency of it all.

"Godammit, man, how did ya fix that? It was like they were expecting me."

Playing it cool, I just said I had a contact.

We arrived at the studio in good shape to find Steve already there. Ken was still amazed by the customs situation. He turned to Steve and told him that he couldn't believe how brilliantly I'd fixed it at the airport. Steve gave me a knowing look.

After that ,it was plain sailing. The word spread like wild fire that Cat Stevens was in town with these top session guys from the US. For the whole time we were recording, there was always a crowd outside the studios wanting to chat. Better still, we had virtual freedom of the town. Everywhere we went, people stopped us and said: "Hey man, what's happnin'?"

It was inevitable that, at some point, someone would chirp up that a smoke was in order. Naturally, I was given the task of organising it. I thought it shouldn't be a problem as we were at the centre of the spliff universe. So, cornering one of the guys who worked at the studios, I asked whether he could get some weed. "No problem, man, I can get you some of the best in town," he assured me.

I thought $20 would be enough for an ounce as that was the going rate in the US at the time, so I gave him the money and off he went. A couple of hours later he came back and handed me a sackful of weed. I could have fallen through the floor! Needless to say, we never got through it all, despite being regular smokers.

When we left Kingston, I handed it on to the guys in the studio. They were delighted and so were we. **CM**

The great escape

Being on the road with Cat Stevens and living a five-star lifestyle, something interesting was always around the corner.

We were performing in Los Angeles and staying at the Beverly Wilshire Hotel, one of the top accommodations for the movie industry. I had to go over to A&M Records to drop off some backstage passes for Jerry Moss, the founder and boss of the label along with trumpeter Herb Albert. They and their entourage were coming to the concert and were all on the VIP guest list. I had liberated Cat's limo for a while and took the liberty of doing some shopping en route, which made me late for a meeting in the hotel bar to work out some production issues.

In a hurry, I made a beeline for an elevator that was just about to go up. I dashed in just as the doors closed and apologised as I nearly bumped into the only other rider.

I pushed the button to my floor and notice that his pressed button was all the way at the top.

Arriving at my floor, I waited for the doors to open. No go. I pressed more buttons. Still nothing. "Bollocks," I said, turning to my fellow passenger. "I think we're stuck."

He started thumping the buttons as well, then picked up the emergency phone to ask for help. "Someone will be there as soon as we can get an engineer," said the reception desk.

It was then that I realised I was trapped in the lift with acting legend Steve McQueen, star of Bullitt, The Magnificent Seven and other huge movies.

He picked up my Brit accent. "What you doing in town?" he asked as we whiled away our time, awaiting rescue. It was a fair question – if you were staying at the Wilshire, you were doing something of note.

"I'm with Cat Stevens. We're doing a show in town," I replied.

"Hey OK, I like his music," he mused.

"Are you going?" I asked.

"Wouldn't mind," he said, at which point I pulled out a couple of complementary tickets and gave them to him.

"Hey, thanks man. I'll try to make it." Film stars love a freebie.

At which point, the doors were prised open and we went our separate ways.

I made it to the bar and apologised to the guys for being late. Being a bit blasé, I added: "I was stuck in a lift with Steve McQueen."

"Yeah, sure," returned a chorus from the crowd. Nobody believed me.

However, later that evening, McQueen actually turned up at the show and it was mentioned that he had been spotted in the audience.

It was only later that it occurred to me how ironic it was to get trapped in a lift with someone whose best-known movie was The Great Escape. And, for that matter, The Towering Inferno!
CM

John Lennon denied party entry

We were gigging on the East Coast and we were driving to the New York venue in Cat Steven's limo. Steve turned to me with an idea: "Let's have a party when we get back after the show tonight. Can you organise it?"

"Sure," I said, slightly panicking. How was I going to get that together at such short notice?

I know. JP will sort it!

I'd known Jimmy Pullis for about six or seven years by then and had taken every artist I had worked with to his venue. He had done very well out of me. Like The Speakeasy in London, JP's was the place to go in New York during the 1970s. It was exclusive to the music business and the names of the artists who went there was a who's who of rock 'n' roll. It was situated on 1st Avenue and East 77th street on the Upper East Side. Apart from being the best place to go and chill, it also had a great reputation for super jam sessions. The likes of James Taylor and Billy Joel were among the scores of artists I saw get up and play in there.

Another thing Jimmy's was known for – if you were one of the select few and I was – was the cellar. That was where the real mischief took place. You could spliff up and were always assured of the best Peruvian marching powder. There was always plenty of it down there. It seemed to just appear and seemingly gratis.

Arriving at the venue, I got on the phone: "Jim, Cat wants a party tonight. Can you do it for us?"

"Sure, anything for you, my man."

The show ended brilliantly and Cat was in a great mood. I walked into his dressing room.

"Is the party on?" he asked.

"You bet. I got it together at JP's."

"Great," he said. "Invite everybody."

Now that was a lot of bodies. The entire band, crew, management and entourage. In addition, a few uptown ladies appeared courtesy of JP. The place was absolutely rammed – you couldn't physically get any more people in.

The party was swinging and I was at the bar in a champagne and weed-induced haze, talking rubbish to all and sundry. JP came over and asked me if I could watch the door for ten minutes as he needed to take care of a little bit of business downstairs. During this time, someone must have pointed me out as having the guest list as a guy I didn't recognise came over and asked if it was OK to come in. I mumbled to him that he would have to wait until JP returned. He got the hump and left immediately left, but a couple of his crowd hung around.

However, that wasn't the end of it. I don't know who it was, but someone told Cat that I had thrown John Lennon out of his party. He was majorly pissed off with me and we had a huge row. Eventually everything got sorted out between us, but it went down in legend that I was the person who had refused entry to John Lennon.

I knew I was out of it and would have never have intentionally thrown him out. I was a big fan. It was two things that had stopped me from recognising him – three things if you include the drink and drugs. First, the lady he was with wasn't Yoko, and second, the guy who stormed off had a shaved head.

Like everybody else, I was used to seeing Lennon with glasses and long hair. On the night, this chap looked completely different. Sod's law, he would come to our bash just after he shaved his head. How was I supposed to know?

So John, wherever you are, if it really was you, I apologise.

CM

Meeting Jock

I first met my great pal to be Malcolm 'Jock' McLean on my first tour of the US with Cat Stevens.

We had flown into LA to start the tour. In the band at that time was Steve, Alun Davies, Larry Steele and new kid Gerry Conway on drums. We checked into the Chateau Marmont on Sunset Strip. The hotel is perched on a hill overlooking Sunset Boulevard and has been a bastion of old Hollywood for many moons. Just about every movie star had stayed there at one time or another: Marilyn Monroe, James Dean, Bette Davis, the list is endless.

We all got settled in and I sauntered down to reception. "Has a Mr McLean checked in yet?" I inquired. He had and was in the parking lot.

Despite his Scottish sounding name, Jock was from the east coast, living in New York. His family home was in Long Island and they came from old money, as they say.

Jock had met Steve while previously working with James Taylor. James and Steve shared the same US management company run by Peter Asher, best-known as one half of vocal duo Peter and Gordon, on the west coast and by Nat Weiss on the east. Nat was the US representative of George Harrison and had been involved with The Beatles.

I went down to the parking lot as a red Pontiac convertible came screeching to an emergency stop right in front of me. "You Carl?" asked the long haired driver, resembling Old West folk hero Wild Bill Hickok (we both had long hair, it took one to know one!).

"Yeah, you Jock?" I replied eyeing the flash wheels.

"Hey man, you wanna go for a ride?" he said puffing on a Marlboro.

"Cool, let's go!" I jumped in.

So off we went, chatting about the tour. We drove around Beverly Hills with the roof down. We turned down Rodeo Drive and I spotted two beautiful Californian ladies.

"Pull over, man."

Jock stopped.

As they passed by I switched into the Queen's English: "Lovely day, girls. Going anywhere special?"

"Nah, just picking up some things. Are you Australian?" they asked.

"No, English."

"Oh wow," they said in unison.

We were heading for some trendy new bar that Jock knew. "Would you like to come along?"

"Sure, OK." They jumped in.

Needless to say we had a jolly good afternoon.

"Goddam man, that was slick. You're my man," Jock said later, as we slapped hands.

Later on the tour, we were running late for a domestic flight. We arrived at the very busy airport and ushered the band straight down to the gate towards the flight.

Jock had previously designated himself quartermaster in charge of weed. He used to keep it and other items in a canvas bag that he simply slung over his shoulder. We called it his drop-out bag.

We managed to get everyone checked in for the flight, but its departure was imminent, so I told Jock to leg it as fast as he could and that I would be right behind him. Off we dashed, dodging people on the way.

All of a sudden, I spotted a trickle falling out of Jock's bag. The trickle soon became a flow as weed fell out all over the concourse.

"Jock, Jock, hold it," I whispered, trying to be discreet.

He stopped and turned around. "Damn it, what's up?"

"The fucking grass, man. It's all fallen out!"

He looked around and turned pale. "Holy cow," he muttered.

"Quick, kick it around sparsely and let's bugger off."

We quickly scuffled around as if we were practicing a strange dance move, before we made a dash for it. We finally arrived at the departure gate and handed out the boarding passes, as we shooed the band on to the plane like we were herding chickens. It was lucky that the authorities never cottoned on, but the bummer was that half the contents of the drop-out bag was gone. Luckily, we managed to procure a new source. **CM**

Carole King owes it all to blackberry brandy

You could say that it was thanks to a bottle of blackberry brandy and me that the legend that is Carole King became a singer.

Picture this. It's 1970. I was tour manager with for King's great friend James Taylor, a major figure in the folk revolution in the United States in the 1960s and early 1970s. His big hits included Carolina On My Mind and the King-penned smash hit You've Got A Friend. We were touring the States at the time.

King had enjoyed minor success with a couple of singles as a performer in the early 1960s, such as It Might As Well Rain Until September, but her attempts at singing live were severely hampered because she suffered from stage fright. Instead, she was having massive success as a songwriter with Aretha Franklin's (You Make Me Feel) Like A Natural Woman, The Monkees' Pleasant Valley Sunday, The Drifters' Up On The Roof, The Locomotion for Little Eva – her former babysitter – and I'm Into Something Good for Earl-Jean McCrea and later covered by Herman's Hermits, to name but a few from a huge songbook of hits.

King was also part of Taylor's band, playing keyboards, her stage fright not affecting her unless she was at the front of the stage. The two of them really got along and were genuinely good friends.

As I said, being at the back of the stage on keyboards as opposed to being at the front singing, suited King at this time. It was crazy to think that despite her being armed with stunning looks, long curly fair hair and a gorgeous smile – not to mention brilliant songs and a great voice – she could be affected in this way, but it was a fact.

That was until one particular day…

We all arrived in the midwest for a gig at the Saint Louis Ambassador Theatre, an elaborate six-storey French Renaissance-style venue that sadly closed for concert in 1976. There must have been about 35 or so of us in the crew and we were lugging the band's equipment and belongings around the country on the roofs of a convoy of beaten-up station wagons. We unloaded all the kit and the crew took care of the sound check. Everything was cool.

Next thing we knew, the promoter was in total meltdown. The headline act had cancelled. It was possibly Joni Mitchell at the top of the bill, but I can't be sure. The problem now, of course, was that the 3,000 fans that were set to pack out the theatre later that night would be rightfully expecting a one-and-a-half hour set. Now expected to headline, Taylor only had something like 55 minutes of music rehearsed and ready for live performing. What could be done to save the day?

Standing right next to James Taylor was Carole King, the woman who had written a stack of brilliant songs that had gone on to become massive selling hits. Unsurprisingly, Taylor turned to her and said, given all that great material up her sleeve, she should go out as a singer. King was understandably reluctant, particularly having been dropped on her at such short notice. She explained that she wasn't expecting to perform vocals and hadn't fronted for years. Finally, like the good sport she was, she agreed., most probably because of her closeness to Taylor and knowing she would be helping him out. If anyone else had asked her, I'm pretty sure she would have turned them down.

Later, with the minutes ticking by and showtime approaching, her nerves were really beginning to get the better of her. She was visibly nervous, practically shaking, with the colour drained from her face. I wasn't sure she was going to make it out on stage. She was not looking good.

With fears rising in the camp about whether Carole would be physically and mentally capable of performing, I had to think of a solution and fast. The only thing I could think that might help numb her fears was necking some hard liquor. Trouble was, I didn't have anything to hand… except for a bottle of blackberry brandy.

Who knew why I had it? I didn't even like the stuff or knew anyone who did. Anyway, I gave her the bottle and encouraged her to have some. She began knocking back a few gulps of the booze. A good few pulls later, the brandy began to kick in.

It certainly did the trick. She stopped shaking and the colour returned to her face. She had a dose of Dutch courage coursing through her veins. There was relief all round, as she confirmed she was OK to go out.

Nerves pushed to one side and with the crowd growing increasingly expectant, she took a few final sips, a number of really deep breaths and walked out up the steps and onto the stage. She looked great; she was wearing flared jeans and a bright red mohair sweater. She performed 30 minutes of her hits and, despite the change of performers, the crowd went crazy – they loved her.

Taylor came on afterwards and he too had a great show. The gig was a total success and that evening really was a watershed for King. Not only did she save the day, she banished a large chunk of her stage fright – or, at least, learned how to deal with her phobia (without the need for blackberry brandy!).

From that day on, James really encouraged Carole to continue being a singer. He became a great source of support to her and helped her continue to beat her anxieties surrounding singing live. Just a year later, in 1971, she released the massively successful album Tapestry, which went on to sell 22 million copies. She really exploded onto the scene as a performer in her own right.

I'm not sure her fans can ever thank Taylor enough for continuously supporting King's singing career, but I also like to think me and my bottle of blackberry brandy contributed in some small way. **JM**

George Harrison meets a fan

It was 1969 and I was with George Harrison and some of the crew that had only a year earlier finished working on one of the greatest albums every released: The Beatles' White Album. We were in the recording studio at the Capital Records building on Yucca and Argyle in Hollywood, where George was recording with fellow Scouser Jackie Lomax – i believe it was a session for the single How The Web Was Woven.

Harrison and Paul McCartney both loved Lomax, certainly enough for them to back him as producer and record company executive at various points in their careers. It's a mystery why Lomax never got to be as well known as his Liverpool contemporaries.

On one particular night, we were recording really late into the evening. We were all getting really hungry, so we strolled over to Ben Franklin's restaurant on Sunset Boulevard for something to eat. It was all pretty low-key, until it was time to pay the bill. We got up to leave and left a tip. At that point, one of the waitresses spotted George: "Hey, aren't you George Hamilton IV? Can I have your autograph?"

Considering he was in the biggest band the world has ever seen, he was so cool and unaffected. He never flinched. "Sure, no problem."

She handed him pen and paper and he proceeded to sign the autograph as country and western singer George Hamilton IV. She was thrilled, totally oblivious to the fact that one of The Beatles had just signed an autograph for her. **JM**

Ringo and George hang out

Ringo Starr and George Harrison were hanging out in Pebble Beach, California.

It was 1968 and around the time the guys were working with Indian musician and spiritual guru Ravi Shankar on the West Meets East experiment, where Shankar introduced traditional Indian instruments to Western artists including The Beatles.

Ringo and George wanted to go and hang out in LA, so we set off on Route 101 down the coast from San Francisco to Los Angeles in two Lincoln Continentals, one white and the other black.

The Lincoln Continental was the car of the time. This was the car that the president of the time, Lyndon B Johnson, was driving around in. In fact he would drive the same route as us when he was in the same area. We were the president in these cars; we got to pretend at least. The Beatles pretending to be the president - I'm sure some presidents have pretended to be The Beatles too!

After three or four hours on the road, we pulled into a diner for something to eat. At the side of the diner was a banqueting hall, where there was some kind of teenage dance going on, with loads of 18 year olds having a great time.

Ringo and the gang found some tables in the diner, in the middle of the floor. We were all with wives and girlfriends and we ordered some food. The teenagers had to walk by the counter and past our tables to get to the toilets, so there was this steady stream of foot traffic going backwards and forwards through the meal.

During the whole time we were sitting down, none of the teenagers picked up on the fact that most of our group were speaking with Limey accents or suspect anything with the food orders, despite the fact that The Beatles and the crew were all pretty much on vegetarian diets – not common back then. There were certainly no burgers or fries being ordered.

After the meal, we settled up and got in the cars and were setting off. At this point, someone finally spotted that there were Beatles in the house. The teenagers suddenly began pouring out of the diner in hysterics as we were pulling away. But it was too late, we were gone!

Funny to think that most of the 200 or so party monsters had walked straight past the tables where the most famous band in the world were eating over a period of about one-and-a-half hours and not one of them had cottoned on.

We got to enjoy our food in peace though, which was great.
JM

Kiss coffin better

Glam rock legends Kiss were doing a pay-per-view concert for the Showtime network. Prior to the gig, the band filmed a behind-the-scenes special to go out as part of the package. After filming, they flew to Pennsylvania for another gig .

I was on board and chatting to vocalist and bass player Gene Simmons during the flight. Gene was on form, as usual, coming up with an idea a minute to earn his next million dollars. We were all goofing around when he came up with the idea of commissioning and launching the Kiss Kasket, complete with the signatures of the four band members on it. He explained that the coffin would also to have a power line and a beer cooler inside.

The idea was that the owner would be able to use the waterproof Kasket as a giant cooler to enable you to rock 'n' roll all night long, then, when their time was up, they could be buried in it. Of course we were all laughing about the idea and nobody was taking Gene's idea seriously. But he had a vision and continued to explain: "It will cost $3,000, but a deluxe version will cost an extra $800 as it would be complete with an LED screen."

Sure enough, Simmons brought the coffin, complete with the Kiss name and logo, to market in 2001. I believe it had a launch price of $4,500 and $5,000 for a signed version. These things have been in production ever since. It is a real coffin, decorated with pictures of the band. They have sold plenty. It has been a real success.

Pantera guitarist 'Dimebag' Darrell Abbott, who was a massive fan and had a Kiss tattoo, was even buried in one after he was tragically killed. His brother Vinnie Paul, drummer of Pantera and Hellyeah, was also buried in a Kiss Kasket at his funeral in 2018.

You've got to admire Gene's entrepreneurial spirit. The band has released some spectacular merchandise over the years – dolls, lunchboxes, belt buckles and toys – but the Kasket remains their greatest innovation. **JM**

Led Zeppelin cash in and crash out

Led Zeppelin were on a massive tour of the United States in 1973. I was tour manager with Cat Stevens at the same time and both bands were staying at the palatial Drake Hotel in Manhattan. It was quite common to be familiar with other road crews back then, as bands crossed paths all the time. You would be playing different venues in the same town at the same time, often staying in the same hotels or travelling on the same aircraft. It was the golden age of touring and there was a real industry gang feeling – everyone knew everyone.

At that time there was no bigger draw on the live circuit than Led Zeppelin. Despite not releasing singles, songs such as Stairway To Heaven, Whole Lotta Love, The Immigrant Song, Dazed And Confused, Communication Breakdown and Kashmir have become timeless classics. The Led Zep odyssey ended in 1980 when drummer John Bonham died at the criminally young age of just 32 years old after one too many booze benders, having suffered alcohol problems for years.

My counterpart with Led Zeppelin was Richard Cole, who looked every bit the part of the hard rock tour manager with his long brown hair and a chiselled moustache and beard. He had worked with the band from their formation in 1968 all the way through the massive highs until he was fired shortly before the group disbanded in 1980.

While working with Zeppelin, Cole was a proven innovator. He was the first tour manager to take British crews on the road in the US. Before him, bands used to hire all their equipment and crew in America. Cole's practice worked better and went on to become the template for the majority of other British bands touring the US. But while he was innovative and talented, Cole was also a wild child. His drink and drug abuse were as legendary as his bosses and it was his relentless partying that eventually got him fired by the band's manager, Peter Grant, on what turned out to be the band's last ever European concert tour. Soon after, he checked into rehab to kick his addictions.

There are some who believe Cole was too close to the band and that he had contributed to Bonham's drinking problems and guitarist Jimmy Page's cocaine and heroin habits. Whether or not this was the case, his friendship with the group definitely saved him from being fired years earlier, after a serious load of the band's gig money went missing.

Don't get me wrong, I'm not saying Cole took the money, but he was the last person to see the cash and he really couldn't have complained too hard had he been booted out.

The controversy arose after Zep had played a steamroller set in front of 20,000 fans at a sold-out Madison Square Garden, one of three gigs that were filmed and later released as the movie The Song Remains The Same in 1976. After the show, the usual stuff was going on backstage: drinks and drugs and girls were all around and everyone in the crew was happy and relaxed as they let off steam.

While the party was in full flow, the band's management received the gig money from the Madison Square Garden box office and it was, in turn, given to Cole as usual. He headed off from the gig to the Drake, a few blocks away, and deposited it in their safe overnight – the correct and normal thing to do. Further partying went on into the small hours at the hotel, until everyone crashed out.

Next morning, Cole's mood was quickly to change. He sauntered downstairs and made his way to the hotel management office, so he could unlock the safe and pick up the cash. He found a couple of hotel staff who were senior enough to unlock the safe for him. Out came the keys and they opened the door. To Cole's complete and utter horror, all of the cash had gone – every last dollar. The haul was around $75,000, a lot of money even now.

The remaining colour drained away from Cole's already peaky and hungover face as the reality of the situation hit home. He demanded answers from the hotel management and he wanted them fast. The trouble was the hotel staff were also totally in shock and there was no paper trail. They were extremely apologetic, but insisted they knew nothing about the missing money or who might have taken it. Of course, this was in the early 1970s before CCTV was in use, so here was nothing that could be done. Cole had no choice but to round up the band and their management to make the embarrassing and serious admission. He told them everything he knew.

Luckily for him, the band believed his story. In fact, they were really good about it. In the end, they told Cole not to worry and that his job was (pardon the pun) safe, albeit he had to endure mockery whenever the subject was raised from then on.

One of the only things that saved his arse that day was the great relationship he had with the band, who trusted him implicitly, and the fact he was bloody good at his job. And at least the passports of the band had been spared. **JM**

John Cooper Clarke to the rescue

Towards the end of the 1970s, Cat Stevens informed us all of his intention to follow his Muslim faith and relinquish his music career. We only half believed him to begin with, however the penny finally dropped with me and I was once again looking for another gig.

A year or so previously, my very good friend Jock McLean had left James Taylor for a newly created department at CBS records in New York, which was to be known as Artist Development. Jock knew the situation with Cat and said to me that the London office was thinking of opening one of their own and he said I would be ideal for it.

He got back to me and told me that it was all on and I should contact managing director Maurice Oberstein. I went along for the interview, it went well and I was in. Not long after

I joined the company, it dawned on me that I was the only person with any hands-on experience of touring and concert promotion – everyone else was fresh out of college or sixth form and the nearest they had got was booking a band for their student union.

To be fair, there were a couple of musicians in the A&R department, namely Steve Winwood's brother Muff and Kenny Loggins' brother Dan, but those guys had never toured on any scale – at best they had gigged in small clubs or pubs.

Consequently it was hard going when it came to marketing and promotion meetings, trying to explain the logistics of being on the road for months on end and why artists in other time zones couldn't do interviews at suggested time. It was very frustrating. I'm sure some of them thought I was being a deliberate pain in the arse.

It all made a bit more sense to me after a meeting with punk poet John Cooper Clarke, who was going on the road supporting The Clash. I had arranged to meet him prior to the tour to explain what to expect and outline the rules of engagement. We then had to attend a dreaded marketing and promotions meeting, which dragged on so much that John glazed over.

After the meeting, we went back to my office. "You know what John, I don't know about you, but I hadn't a bloody idea what that meeting was all about," I revealed.

He looked at me wryly and said in his broad Mancunian accent: "Ye know wha' Carl, they've all got t'fucking illusions of inadequacy, but don't worry, 'cos next week we're gonna have a meeting about a fucking meeting."

I cracked up… and marketing meetings made much more sense thereafter. And his inversion of the usual 'delusions of grandeur' has stayed with me ever since. I still smile every time I think of it.   **CM**

Judas Priest: sheer Hart attack

Vocalist and lead guitarist Lea Hart supported Judas Priest on our 1979 Killing Machine tour of the UK and was well known for being a bit of a wag. Coupled with the fact that the last night of any tour was always the most likely night for wind-ups, you could pretty much guarantee he'd have something up his sleeve.

So as the gig came to a climax, we prepared to launch into our last song of the set. Unknown to us, Lea had taped the same song from the previous night.

So there we were, triumphant from just about completing the tour, with just the last song to play out. The crowd were buzzing and expectant there would be one final hurrah.

As we prepared to strike the opening chord, Lea got in ahead of us and began playing the recording from the previous night through the sound system, leaving the band fumbling around trying to catch up.

We started to mime along along with the recording and actually seemed to get away with it for a while. However, just when it seemed we were in the clear, the road crew jumped on stage and started taking all the equipment away a bit at a time. The snare drum and the amps went first, while the rest soon followed as we were still trying desperately to mime to the end of the track!

Another favourite prank by the road crew was to sprinkle talcum powder on the drumheads before we came out on stage. The band, and especially the drummer, could never tell… until it was too late. The moment one of our drummers first struck the drums he would get absolutely covered in the stuff, but would just have to carry on, immersed in a cloud of powder. And, of course, the hotter and sweatier he got, the more the talc would stick to him. **IH**

Judas Priest: KK out of his depth

KK Downing, the guitarist in Judas Priest, and water just didn't mix. He was a pathetic swimmer and he hated being near any body of water.

To illustrate just how much Ken and water didn't go together, I'll give you a few examples.

One time I remember I had to save him while he was having a swimming lesson in a pool. For a laugh, Carl, our road manager, had told him to jump in at the deep end – and he only went and did it, with obvious results.

Another time we were caught out by a severe flash flood while driving across America. Flash floods in Texas can and often do wreak severe damage. I mean the rain just came pouring down, like nothing I have ever seen before or since. The car we were driving was literally starting to float along the freeway.

Needless to say, Ken was not happy with the situation and started panicking and shouting "Stop the car! Stop the car! I'm getting out!" He opened the door and leapt out. All we heard was this 'plop' noise as he sank into the floodwater, a few feet deep. For a split second he was gone, only to re-emerge, soaked through, moments later. We all cracked up.

With this in mind, it is all the more amazing that I once witnessed Ken save a woman from drowning in Birkenhead. He even won a community award for it.

It all happened during a tall ship ceremony at the Liverpool port. Ken had a friend who had rented a boat for the band to watch the event from the water. So we came sailing merrily round into Birkenhead harbour, near where the ferries come in. We jumped ashore and had a walk around, inspecting the boats and soaking up the atmosphere. After a really pleasant time, we returned to the hired boat and it was then that the incident took place. An inexperienced woman had slipped on the harbour side as she was clambering around and fallen into the water not far from where our boat was moored.

At the back of our boat there was a small dinghy attached by a rope. Quick as a flash, Ken selflessly jumped into the dinghy, untied the rope and rowed straight out to the woman, pulling her out of the drink.

Like I say, it was exceptionally brave because Ken would have really been in trouble himself had he fallen in. The lady was fine in the end and was extremely thankful. Ken got many pats on the back that day.　**IH**

Judas Priest: who the fuck is Tom Cruise?

It was 1986 and Judas Priest was putting the finishing touches to the Turbo album. While in the studio and completely out of the blue, we got a call from the top brass over at Paramount Pictures. They basically wanted to use the song Reckless from our yet-to-be-completed album on the soundtrack to some movie called Top Gun starring a young actor named Tom Cruise.

Now you have to remember that, at that point, Tom Cruise was not the global superstar he is today. He'd earned decent notices for playing the lead in the raunchy comedy Risky Business three years earlier, but his last movie – the fairytale fantasy Legend – had bombed at the box office. None of the band had seen Risky Business so we simply didn't know who the fuck Tom Cruise was or believe that Top Gun would be a hit.

Anyway, Paramount were putting the soundtrack together and had already lined up Berlin with Take My Breath Away, Kenny Loggins with Danger Zone and The Righteous Brothers with You've Lost That Lovin' Feeling. Unknown to us at the time, they had also approached Bryan Adams about using his song Only The Strong Survive, but he had turned them down because he felt the film would glorify war.

We probably would have let them use Reckless, but for the fact they wanted exclusive rights to the song. The deal was that it was either gonna go appear on their soundtrack album or on Turbo, but not on both. So we said "Fuck it, we'll keep it on our album."

In hindsight, we probably made the wrong move, didn't we? The Paramount guys said they were going to play the song at the point in the film when Cruise's Maverick takes off on his motorcycle after his best mate Goose, played by Anthony Edwards, has been killed. It was all very emotional and full of testosterone.

Top Gun not only turned out to be the box office smash of the summer, but the soundtrack was a number one album and stayed at the top of the charts for fucking months, shifting more than nine million copies in the US alone. To this day, it remains one of the top ten biggest-selling movie soundtracks ever.

To add insult to injury, two years later we contributed a cover version of the Chuck Berry classic Johnny B Goode to the movie of the same name, a low budget teen comedy about a high school student chasing a sports scholarship. At the time, we were thinking that we didn't want to get caught out again, only for the film to be a complete and utter flop. We were all like "Fucking typical!"

Some you win, some you don't. Except we lost out both times.

IH

Iron Maiden and Judas Priest: what happens in Vegas

I'll never forget hanging out with my old pal Dicky Bell in Las Vegas, while touring with Iron Maiden and Judas Priest. I was there with Maiden and he was with Priest. Coincidentally, I also knew Judas Priest well as I had tour managed their first ever US tour. We were all from the Midlands and they were all-round good chaps. Ian Hill from Priest remains one of my best mates to this day.

It was very rare to work on a tour when you knew both bands;, but it made for a very smooth operation. However, this particular gig happened to be in Vegas, which was always a recipe for trouble.

The show went well as per normal and afterwards we all went back to the hotel, which also housed a casino and, like most hotels on the Vegas strip, was open all night.

So there I am looking around this chintzy hotel for Dicky Bell. After wading endlessly through a maze of slot machines, I bumped into a couple of his crew.

"Have you seen Dick?"

"Yeah, he's on the tables. Don't think he's doing well though," they warned.

Shaking my head and cursing under my breath, I finally spotted him.

"Dick ,what's happnin' man. You winning?"

"Bit down at the minute, Carl," he slurred as a hostess handed him another short. He carried on chucking chips on the table.

After watching Dick downing shorts and dumping more chips for a while, I got a bit bored and thought about wandering off for a bit more excitement.

"Come on, man, let's split and find some action. There's crumpet at the bar."

By now Dick was a little unsteady on his feet. "No man, I'll catch you later. Gotta try and get my dough back."

"OK. If not, I'll see you for breakfast." There was no answer from Dick apart from an inebriated wave, so off I went.

At breakfast the next morning, in walked Dick, looking a bit worse for wear. He slumped at the table, head in his hands and sat in total silence.

"What's up, man? How did you do in the end?" I asked.

"It all went a bit wrong," he admitted with a worried look on his ashen face. "I fucked up a bit."

"What do you mean?"

"Blew all my money," he groaned.

"Oh well! I told you to leave it out," I said I righteously.

Looking at me guiltily way, he continued. "That's not all. I blew the band's money as well."

"What do you mean?" I said in total disbelief.

"The band's money. The float. What am I going to do?"

I gave it to him straight: "The only thing you can do is tell the band and tell them you'll pay a bit back at a time. They'll be OK. They're cool. They'll just say you're a prat."

He took my advice and the band was cool about it. But I don't think Dick has ever returned to the tables since. **CM**

Iron Maiden: lost and found

While on the hunt for a new gig in 1975, I trawled through my network of contacts and learned that EMI had high hopes for a young heavy metal band they had just signed. The label was set to put its weight and considerable investment behind a band called Iron Maiden. I was told to contact Maiden's manager, Rod Smallwood, to arrange a meeting. We met a little while later and got on quite well.

Rod explained that Maiden were going to do a world tour, taking in Europe, America and Japan. It was going to be a mix of clubs and support slots for the likes of Kiss, Judas Priest and others, and EMI would be underwriting the costs.

"Could you set the tour up?" Rob asked.

I said I could, but would want a free hand. Rod agreed, especially after I told him I'd run Judas Priest's US tour a couple of years earlier.

The band at the time consisted of Steve Harris, Paul Di Anno, Adrian Smith, Dave Murray and Clive Burr. We got on well despite me not being a big metal fan, not to mention me being and an Aston Villa supporter and them being West Ham fanatics. The guys were always up for some fun and had that typical East End of London sense of humour, especially Clive, who constantly buzzed me with all sorts of questions about the places we were scheduled to tour. I don't think any of the band had been out of the UK at that point and they were fascinated by stories of different cultures.

The tour went ahead smoothly and the shows were great. The European leg over, we set off for Japan and checked in at the Tokyo Hilton a couple of days before the first show. The first question the band asked was "What are we going to do? Where's the action?"

I said I'd have a word with the promoter and arrange something. I knew the promoter quite well from previous tours and arranged some afternoon and evening activities, starting in Ginza, a huge shopping area in Tokyo, full of stores that sold all the latest electronic gadgets. This was to be followed by a session in a vast amusement arcade where we could play virtual golf and clay pigeon shooting.

At Ginza, everyone went wild, buying all sorts of gadgets and trivia. especially Clive who seemed to buy the entire shop. Cameras, games, toys – you name it, he bought it. He had to buy a massive holdall to carry everything.

Next stop, the arcade. The guys played everything they could, stuffing Yen into every slot on offer. After a couple of hours I rounded them up and we headed back to the hotel, ahead of the evening's loony shindigs.

Back at the Hilton, I figured that I would slink off to my room to get some respite and relief from the high energy bunch, before heading off to sample the decadent Tokyo nightlife. I was just about to escape when I heard my name shouted out. Clive came haring across the hotel lobby pushing past other hotel guests.

"I've lost me swag! I've lost me swag!" he wailed, in full meltdown mode.

"What do you mean you've lost your swag?" I said bemused.

"I think I left it at the arcade. What am I going to do? It cost me a bleeding packet!"

"You cockney berk, how much did you spend?"

"A good couple of grand," he admitted.

"What, Yen?"

"No, fucking dollars, man," he cried.

"You divot! Come with your Uncle Carl," I said in a mock condescending manner.

I frogmarched him back out of the hotel and pushed him into our wheels, where our driver was on stand-by.

"Back to the fucking arcade," I grumbled.

"That's a waste of time," Carl moaned, shoulders hunched in despair. "The stuff will be long gone. Some bastard will have half-inched it by now."

"We'll give it a go. Keep the faith. Trust your Uncle Carl," I said, trying and probably failing to be reassuring.

We arrived back at the arcade and the place was really crowded. I went with Clive to retrace everywhere he had been. We began pushing our way through the crowd to all the games he had played. Eventually and after many 'sumimasens' and 'arigatos' (excuse-mes and thank-yous) we got to another game.

"Have you been on this one?" I shouted to Clive.

"Yeah."

"Well get to the front and check," I bawled at him.

He did… and guess what? The bag was still there, completely untouched. Clive retrieved his swag and was as happy as a four-balled tomcat.

Grinning from ear to ear, he chirped up: "How did you know it was gonna be there?"

I explained: "I was pretty sure. It's their culture, man. They don't like tea leaves here." ('Tea leaf' is Cockney rhyming slang for a thief).

All was well again, and after that Clive always called me Uncle Carl.
CM

The Small Faces: meltdown on the Mexican border

Steve Marriott was one of the very best and most underrated rock vocalists that Britain has ever produced. He came to fame in the mid-1960s when The Small Faces were racking up a string of hits. He then formed Humble Pie with Peter Frampton, who went on to do great things in the United States.

Unfortunately, Marriott developed a really bad reputation as a wild boy. He hit the drugs and booze hard. Added to that, he built up a huge belligerence towards anything and anyone in authority, especially people on the business side of the music industry.

I was a big fan of The Small Faces, especially Steve Marriott, and by chance he happened to be the opening act on a tour I worked on. The line-up included Iron Maiden and Judas Priest. Quirky really, as Marriott was more hard rock than metal.

I was working with Maiden and got to know him quite well – I already knew him by reputation. Back then, who didn't? He had that kind of arrogance and charisma about him coupled with a Dennis the Menace grin, that you couldn't resist.

We were touring in Texas during the summer of 1981. After a gig one night, Steve came over to me: "Hey Charlie, I'm going on the bus with the road crew tonight, mate."

Oh dear. I could smell trouble, but there was no point in saying that it wasn't a good idea to Steve. He'd do it regardless.

They drove down to the next gig, close to the Mexican border. At some point en route, the border patrol decided to pull their bus over. Border patrol was not interested in anything apart from illegal immigrants – that was what their job was all about.

Steve was off his face big time when they boarded the bus to check for 'wetbacks', as they referred to recent crossings of the Rio Grande river. They looked on the bus, underneath it, in the boot, everywhere.

Steve became increasingly agitated. Getting out of his pram, he started screaming: "You fascist bastards! You're all fascist bastards!' Plus a series of other ripe words and phrases. A couple of the crew tried to calm him down, but to no avail.

The officers eventually lost their patience with his increasingly loud vocal onslaught. He was arrested and thrown in jail.

Next day was a show day. No Marriott.

I got the full lowdown from the crew: "It wasn't his fault, man. He was goaded." Of course he was.

I realised it fell to me to have to tell the local promoter. He went ballistic, bawling on about "that asshole". He was forced to go out and give the usual excuses to the audience. Naturally, he got jeered and booed off. Poor chap. Having finally calmed down, he used his influence with the law and got Marriott bailed.

The next show day arrived and Marriott turned up with his usual swagger, five minutes before he was due onstage, as if there was nothing untoward. Looking a bit rough round the edges with his cheeky grin, his Cockney twang could be clearly heard: "Facking coppers. They're all tossers, mate."

He went out on stage and played an absolute blinder.

It was those kinds of experiences that inspired him. How else do you think he could have come up with songs such as 30 Days In The Hole? Marriott certainly proved that heroes could also be villains.   **CM**

Patti La Belle in a hairy situation

Along with Aretha Franklin, Patti La Belle has to be considered one the very best soul singers of all time. Not only that, but Pattie was a pleasure to work with. She was a really lovely, genuine person, very calm and good humoured. She had developed her craft in church choirs and her range was phenomenal – she could crack a window!

In the mid-1980s, Patti was enjoying a new lease of life, with chart hits and a track on the multi-million selling Beverly Hills Cop soundtrack. She came to Europe a number of times during this period and I always looked forward to meeting up with her and the rest of the entourage.

I'll never forget one promotional trip where she was doing the rounds of TV chat shows, radio interviews and print media. One afternoon, I accompanied her to the then-famous BBC studios in London's White City. I enjoyed these outings because it gave me a chance to get to know her better and we could chat and gossip about all sorts of things. Patti loved to chat.

While we were sitting around in her dressing room waiting for the call to go on air, she turned to me. "Carl, honey"– she called everyone honey – "can you pass me the scarf out of my bag?"

"Of course."

I ferreted around and started to pull out sachets of ketchup, mayonnaise, mustard and all sorts of bits and pieces.

"Patti", I asked, "why have you got all of these things in your bag?"

"Honey, I keep that stuff in there 'cos it reminds me of when I first started out, way back. In those days, when we were on the road, a black person couldn't go into some diners, especially in the south. So we always had to use the rear door of the truck stop to get our burgers and do it quick. But damn it, the guys would always forget the relishes. I carry these to remind me of those days."

I was shocked, but I could relate to what she was saying, having toured south of the Mason-Dixon line with The Foundations in the 1960s.

Around this time, Patti also appeared as The Acid Queen in a revival of The Who's rock opera Tommy at The Royal Albert Hall in London, alongside Elton John, Phil Collins and Billy Idol. At the end of one performance there was a huge after-show bash for the cast and guests. I accompanied Patti to the party and we found a spot near the bar. Elton and Billy Idol said hello and congratulated her on a great performance. She was in great spirits, enjoying herself and chatting away to all and sundry.

At some point during the evening I spotted George Harrison on the other side of the room and told Patti. She gushed: "Oh, I'd love to meet him."

"Would you like me to introduce you?" I offered.

I knew George's American attorney, so taking the bit between my teeth, I bowled over to him: "Excuse me ,George, so sorry to interrupt. I'm a friend of Nat's." He knew immediately who I meant – result! "I'm here with Patti La Belle and she would love to meet you. Would you mind saying hello?"

"Sure, that would be great," he said. I recall thinking how diluted his Scouse accent had become.

We walked over and I introduced them. Patti being Patti went right into one and they got on great. That was definitely some goodwill chalked up for me right there.

One of the things Patti was well known for was her love of sky-high, freaked-out wigs. They were an entity unto themselves. She had at least half-a-dozen or so and most were ten or twelve inches tall, in all sorts of bizarre shapes, including multi-coloured Chinese fans. They were custom made and hugely expensive and were treated like children.

They were accompanied by Patti's hairdresser at all times.

They even had a specially-made flight case to house them. Before they could be transported, they all had to be anchored firmly in place and separately. This case was no mean baby. It wasn't particularly heavy, but it was massive. Naturally the wigs travelled first class, just in case.

On one of her European tours, the wigs went on a journey without us. The first couple of gigs went great and everyone appeared to be happy bunnies. The next stop was in Munich. On arrival, Pattie was greeted by fans, press and record executives. Meanwhile, I oversaw the entourage collecting their gear from baggage claim and moved them through customs and into the arrivals area.

All of a sudden, Patti's hairdresser appeared: "Carl, the wig case isn't here."

"Don't worry, it's probably coming round separately," I replied, trying not to show any anxiety. "I'll chase it up. You go to the hotel and I'll see you there."

My true feeling was far less sanguine. Fucking shit, I thought. I dashed to the airline desk. "I've got a missing flight case. It's vitally important. Patti La Belle. Check it out please. And in the meantime, can you get me back to the baggage area so I can look around for it?" I

After a lot of cajoling, I managed to persuade the ground staff to let me back into the customs area. No wig case to be found. Swearing profusely, I returned to the desk.

"Mr Miller, we've found your item."

"Great! Where is it?"

"It's on its way to Singapore."

"Singapore! Oh no! It's vital luggage. I'm desperate."

After much negotiation, I managed to have it sent back to us as a priority, but it was going to take a couple of days. The non-stop flight time to Singapore is 12 hours each way and in those days flights would make several stops en route. It would take days to get the case back.

When I got to the hotel, I knocked on Patti's door. She was with her hairdresser.

Trying to be upbeat, I said: "Hi. It's about the wigs."

"You found them?" Pattie drawled.

"Well, yeah… in Singapore."

"Singapore! Oh my Lord," she said. "We'll have to cancel the show. I can't go on."

I had never seen Patti go full diva before – it came as quite a surprise.

Eventually the dust settled and calm was restored. The team made up a wig from some of her spares and the show went great. Even if it was a little hair-raising for a while.   **CM**

The lure of Tina Turner

The first time I heard the term 'MTV' ever come up in conversation was in 1979, while in the US. I was working on a tour that had been arranged with Jock McLean, my opposite number at CBS.

Jock was a guy of considerable pedigree, going back to working with The Beatles at Shea Stadium, their legendary 1965 gig. CBS had just signed a great new band and had put a tour of the US together for them. The band was Bruce Woolley & the Camera Club.

Bruce had already gained a reputation as a songwriter – he had written Video Killed The Radio Star, a Camera Club track that later became a huge and enduring hit for producer Trevor Horn's band The Buggles. We had high hopes for the band.

During the tour I developed a friendship with bass player Nigel Ross-Scott, who would later join the new wave band Re-Flex. One night, after a gig, Nigel, Jock and I had a few drinks in a raunchy club. Out of the blue, Jock announced that he was moving to Viacom and that they were going to start a new television channel. Nigel and I looked at each other a bit confused, before Nigel started to grill Jock about how it was going to work, the format and so on. Jock was very laid-back and a terrific problem-solver, which is why they were 'stealing' him from us… at least, that is what it felt like at the time.

Initially, I couldn't get my head around the idea of 24/7 music television, as video production had yet to become the huge industry it later did. It just wasn't a thing for most bands at the time. When Jock explained the future he saw for the medium, I was utterly blown away by his vision, but was still sceptical as to whether the world was ready for it. He won me over and kept us utterly enthralled. We almost forgot there was a proper New York rock 'n' roll party roaring away all around us.

The next morning, I thought back through the haze that I must have dreamed it all, but of course I hadn't. Jock moved to MTV and, as we were good pals, we stayed in touch. He kept me in the loop as they got the channel off the ground.

MTV kicked off in the US to huge fanfare. Jock kept telling me that all was going well, but that they were short on product to rotate and, as a result, they were having to repeat a lot of music videos. Not surprising really, as there were only a few short trailers of groups and artists in those days or retro TV clips. The archive stuff, while more plentiful, didn't fit the bill, as MTV was supposed to be a 'now' channel.

Not long after, CBS declared that all of their artists were going to make promotional videos, starting with the major artists and working down. What was exciting about the concept of MTV was that we already understood the power of TV as a selling tool through bands performing on BBC shows such as Top Of The Pops, The Old Grey Whistle Test and Saturday morning kids' shows. A single appearance could send a track right up to the top of the charts.

At the start of the 1980s, very few outfits were shooting promos because there were no regular outlets that didn't demand either live performances or, at least, miming in person. Cost was also a factor. Yet within two years, MTV had made such an impact that making music videos had become the norm. MTV achieved what few businesses ever do: pretty much vertical take-off. Eventually, rival record companies cottoned on and so began a bonanza of video releases that satisfied MTV's appetite for content.

It also spawned a new type of presenter: the video jockey or VJ. Musicians and record companies looked to these people around record release and US tour announcements for their invaluable promotional help and enthusiasm.

Fast-forward a few years and, out of the blue, I got a call from Jock. He told me they were going to launch MTV in Europe. As part of the kick off, they were going to film Tina Turner's Break Every Rule Tour. Jock told me the film crew were inexperienced with rock shows and that, if I was interested, could I act as an independent arbitrator should any issues arise. Of course I said yes. Who would turn down Tina Turner?

The tour went really well. The only issue that arose was with the master tapes of the show and who should take charge of them. Tina's straight-talking Aussie manager Roger Davies was reluctant to let them go, but eventually agreed that I should hold on to them until he was satisfied with the deal.

We arrived in Amsterdam towards the end of the tour and one evening I had dinner with the producer for MTV, an amiable chap called Brian Diamond. During the meal, Brian mentioned to me that they were struggling for VJs and that they wanted fresh faces and definitely no one from radio. He asked whether I knew anyone who fitted the bill. "Funnily enough, I do know someone who would be good," I replied. "A chap called Nigel Ross-Scott. He's a top muso, very articulate and has a great speaking voice and presentation." Brian asked whether I could arrange a meeting.

Nigel was recording with Dexy's Midnight Runners at the time. He got home late one evening and picked up a message to call Amsterdam. "Can you babysit a tape machine over to Hamburg the day after tomorrow?" said my cryptic message. "It'll be to your advantage. Oh, and it's for the Tina Turner tour."

Unfortunately, Nigel got hold of the wrong end of the stick: "I thought – and hoped – they were firing Tina Turner's bass player. So, with completely the wrong impression fixed in my head, I set off for Hamburg."

Nigel got into Hamburg in the late afternoon and found a message to meet me in the hotel bar in half-an-hour. So he showered, changed into 'backstage rags' and went down to the bar, expecting to get straight off to the stadium for the gig. Instead, I told him to relax and have a drink, as we had to do the handover of the tape machine first.

After a short while, a group of Americans appeared through the entrance, all wearing MTV tour jackets and laughing their heads off like they'd just heard the best joke. They all came over and joined us, yelling good-naturedly at the barman to hurry up with the beers:

"We gotta leave half-an-hour ago!"

Nigel picks up the story: "Carl introduced the 'spotter' as a great friend and colleague of Jock's by the name of Brian Diamond. I had already done many interviews and a couple of 'specials' with MTV on various tours of the States and had got to know some of the lead production people there reasonably well. I had already heard Brian's name mentioned, in suitably hushed tones, as their senior Special Projects guy.

"From his reputation, I was expecting someone walking six inches above the floor and wearing wings, so was relieved to meet a young-looking, down to earth, ultra-professional guy with an obvious sense of fun, and a head of hair that reminded me of Scott Gorham from Thin Lizzy' The kind of man you noticed when he walked into a room.

"By this time, MTV was a primal force in the global music business – the 'go to' organisation to get your musical message out there and revered worldwide. Since launch, they had completely changed the game – if they playlisted a video, the track got traction. It was therefore quite an honour to be in such company.

"The rest of Brian's team had disappeared to get changed for the evening, but we continued to chat away. He didn't seem overly concerned by the passage of time, so I asked when we were going to the gig, as I was really keen to see how they mounted a live shoot of that size. Brian and Carl laughed as they explained that they were actually there to film a planeload of US competition winners, all big Tina Turner fans, who were meeting Tina post-gig and heading off to dinner, so they were only running three cameras. This was the first time they had ever done this, hence Brian's presence as the head of Special Projects.

"On a prompt from Carl, which I found a bit strange, Brian started to ask about my history, how I got into the business, who I had played with before Re-Flex and what I was up to now, immediately followed by 'What's the weirdest gig you've ever done?'

Now that was actually a 'stock' question often asked by the New York VJs, so I should have twigged what was up at that point. It's also a very difficult question for me to answer as I've done quite a few!

"In 1984, Re-Flex played as special guests on the US leg of The Police's Synchronicity tour, building on our success with The Politics Of Dancing album in the States. Some of these gigs were huge and one was at the Atlanta Braves stadium, a sold-out 76,000 capacity show. All afternoon prior to the gig, we'd been doing radio and local TV promotion and had heard a rumour that there were up to 20,000 forged tickets out on the streets. We interpreted that as a compliment and moved on, pre-gig adrenaline pumping.

"The first time we realised that the situation with the forged tickets was a very big deal was when we arrived at the venue to find the National Guard in the car park. The entire backstage area was crawling with cops, both uniformed and plain-clothes, with guys wandering about yelling into walkie-talkies and an absolute ban on anyone leaving the secure area, the whole nine yards. We ended up spending most of the time in our dressing room or watching the other support bands do their stuff.

"Stage time came and on we went. The gig was being filmed for a DVD, so the side stage area was full of camera crews, which made us feel pretty special, even though we weren't the primary subjects. The gig was one of the best we'd ever played, with a standing ovation and cigarette lighters in the air, so we were really buzzing as we came off, only to have our crew guys wrap wet towels around our faces and forcibly usher us straight to our dressing room. We quickly understood why as the smell of teargas was unmistakable!

As it turned out, some of the fans with forged tickets were really upset that they couldn't get in and had decided to take it out on the National Guard, which was not a wise thing to do anywhere, never mind in the USA. It was supremely weird to stand on the side of the stage just a few minutes later, watching one of the biggest bands in the world playing a total blinder, while there was what felt like a war going on outside.

"That was the story I told to Brian. More beer arrived, prompting a visit to the bathroom.

When I returned, Carl had a broad grin all over his face and Brian was nowhere to be seen. I asked what was going on, but Carl didn't want to share the joke, simply saying that Brian would be back shortly and ordered more drinks, still grinning like a Cheshire Cat. Brian duly returned, all business this time. He refused a beer as his car was on its way and I suddenly realised that we'd pretty much missed the gig, which I thought I'd flown over to see.

"Call me stupid, but I still hadn't the first idea of what was actually going on until Carl piped up: 'The poor boy is confused – talk to him.' Brian gave me a very serious look:

'You know the business, you're articulate and you tell a story really well. Once we've put this gig to bed, I'm flying to London in a few days to sort out the final details before we announce the launch of MTV in Europe. You would obviously have to do a screen test, but how would you feel about being a presenter for us?' Boom! The penny finally dropped. Carl nearly fell off his chair laughing and spluttering: 'You should see the look on your face!'

"I think it was John Lennon who once said 'Life is what happens while you're making other plans.' I had flown over to Hamburg at the behest of my best friend, thinking that he was putting me in the frame for a great bass-playing gig. I flew home the next morning feeling that my life might be about to change completely." **CM & NRS**

Sex Pistols darken the mood

The Sex Pistols are one of the most iconic punk bands ever. So imagine my thrill when I was told I would be working with them when they reformed in 2007 to play five nights at London's Brixton Academy. I was going to be a part of their movement… albeit 30 years after it started.

The atmosphere in the Academy was electric and it was truly magical to watch from the side of the stage as these legends performed live once again. John Lydon was full of attitude, anger and expletives. His timing was perfection and his outfits were the right mix of satire and humour, tweed materials and a bleached Mohican – what a combination. Glen Matlock was back on bass. He and Paul Cook produced a rhythm section that was just so perfectly tight. The whole experience was magical.

My only slight regret was being fired by Lydon before the fifth show!

It happened on the afternoon before the fifth gig. John bowled over and asked me to trek out onto Brixton High Street to buy some dark chocolate for him. Not very punk, but I duly obliged. I strolled out into busy and edgy Brixton, the smells of fast food and car exhaust filling my nostrils. I found a newsagent and went in. Twenty minutes later, I retuned to the Academy, complete with confectionery. I went in through the stage door and found Lydon loitering around. "Here you are, Johnny. Here's your chocolate."

He looked at the chocolate before aiming his famous wild-eyed stare straight at me. I began to feel a little uncomfortable, with good reason.

"What the fuckin' hell is this shit?" he snapped.

"It's your chocolate," I replied.

"I asked for fucking dark chocolate! DARK chocolate, not milk chocolate. I'm not having this shit. You're fired. Fuck off, you hear me?" He was almost frothing at the mouth as he pointed me back out through the door I had only just entered.

I was absolutely stunned to be fired from arguably the most anarchic band ever… for buying the wrong kind of chocolate! I sheepishly meandered back towards the stage door and left, uttering under my breath that I never thought the Pistols were as good as The Damned.

Fired by the great man himself, though. That's something to tell the grandkids.   SC

Guns 'n' Roses get Down On The Farm

If you are interested in the science of coincidence then you will share my fascination with how one individual can directly affect another without even knowing it. It's even more intriguing when you realise that a random person has directly affected you – and improved your bank balance into the bargain.

With this in mind, you can imagine how I felt as a songwriter and guitarist to discover how one of the biggest bands of all time had come to cover a tune I had co-written. The song in question was by British punk band the UK Subs. It was called Down On The Farm, which we originally released in 1982 on our Endangered Species album, which contained 14 songs with more of a heavy metal sound than our earlier work.

Founded by singer Charlie Harper, the Subs had a number of UK top 40 singles, including our best known song, Stranglehold. Our biggest selling album was Brand New Age, released in 1980, which reached number 18 in the UK album chart.

The other band in question were the one-time giants of bad boy rock, a band that brought raw rock music back to the mainstream and became the biggest band in the world for several years in the late 1980s. I am referring to the legend that is Guns 'n' Roses.

Their Appetite For Destruction shifted 30 million copies, making it one of the bestselling albums of all time.

The story of how they came to cover Down On The Farm was told to me by their original guitarist, Izzy Stradlin, undeniably a driving force in the band, but often left in the shadows of the raunchy, charismatic singer Axl Rose and brooding gunslinger Slash. The seeds were sown (pardon the pun) for their UK Subs cover way before Guns 'n' Roses were even formed.

A young, talented and determined Izzy and Axl outgrew their Indiana backwater in their late teens, with Izzy heading for the bright lights of Los Angeles. Axl soon followed, leaving behind a whole bunch of trouble into the bargain. His natural father had left the family home and he and his mother had both been abused by his stepfather, Stephen 'Beetle' Bailey. Tearaway Axl had been arrested by local police about 20 times and had struggled to live in a religious family and strict neighbourhood.

The pair of them arrived in LA with pretty much the clothes on their back and guitars in hand and nothing else. They ended up sleeping on a friend's floor and were alleged to have sold drugs for a while to raise some petty cash. This friend of theirs was not at all wealthy either, living in a squalid one-room studio apartment in a piss-poor neighbourhood. Not all of Hollywood is movie stars and millionaires. This guy was also a hardcore junkie, and as serious druggies tend to, he had sold off all his possessions one by one to fund his habit. The TV had gone and so had most of the furniture. He had also sold off what was once a vast and varied record collection for quick and easy dollars.

After a while, he was left with just his favourite two records. Despite his undoubted need and sheer desperation, he steadfastly refused to sell these albums for his next bag of gear.

The first record he had kept was Damaged by hardcore LA punk band Black Flag, famous for their fierce, ferocious and eccentric frontman Henry Rollins. The album was perhaps the best California punk album of its time, full of anger and boredom, with 15 great songs such as TV Party and Six Pack. The second album that survived was Endangered Species.

Every day the junkie would go off and score his drugs or whatever else he did, leaving Axl and Izzy alone in the flat. With nothing to do and no money, they stayed indoors, often listening to the two records over and over They did this for weeks on end. I don't know how they never went stir crazy. Maybe they did.

Axl and Izzy eventually met and joined forces with Slash, Duff McKagan and Steven Adler out of the constantly shifting line-ups of bands in and around the Sunset Strip scene. They signed to Geffen Records in 1987 and the rest is history.

Fast-forward to 1990 and the band was at the height of its fame – giants astride the globe. At the time they were riding high, a crisis in the US agricultural world was unfolding and many family farms were going out of business and folks were losing their livelihoods. Big names such as Guns 'n' Roses, Iggy Pop, Johnny Cash and a host of others were invited to play two songs each at the fourth annual Farm Aid concert organised by Willie Nelson in April 1990, to help raise money and awareness for the farmers, inspired by Live Aid, an fundraising concert that had raised money for famine-stricken Ethiopia in 1985.

Before they went on, Axl was talking to the band backstage about what songs they should play. He and Izzy remembered Down On The Farm and thought it would be perfect. The two of them had played along to the tune over and over again for months in the junkie's flat. They never formally learned it, they just knew it from memory, but they were confident they could carry it off. So they went out on stage in front of thousands of fans and bloody well played it off the cuff. Smashed it, in fact.

Straight after the show, Iggy Pop, for whom I had played bass on many occasions, was the first person to tell me that Guns 'n' Roses had played my song live. He called me up while backstage: "Guess what?" he said in a serious voice. I thought it was going to be bad news, but I got off the phone a few minutes later and started shouting out with joy. What an honour!

The song went down so well with the band and the fans that they decided to put it on their 1993 punk covers album The Spaghetti Incident?, which went on to sell something like seven million copies.

So I had an LA junkie with great taste in music to thank for having that song appear on a Guns 'n' Roses album. Cheers, pal, whoever you are.   **AG**

UK Subs buy £100,000 lager

Did you know that he UK Subs once bought what turned out to be one of the world's most expensive crates of beer?

This story is typical of the music business, where many bands have and will continue to make short-sighted decisions. It tells you a lot about the business acumen of musos and, in particular, UK Subs singer Charlie Harper.

The band was thinking of releasing a single called Tomorrow's Girls because we felt it had crossover potential, thus there was a chance of it being a hit. One night, Charlie went to The Marquee Club in London's West End. Being very excited at the thought of what this single could do for the band, he was at the bar all night talking it up and buying everyone else a drink. As the night wore on, he had splashed his cash and was now skint.

Charlie liked to play host. It was his thing. Being broke was not conducive to playing host, but he spotted music publisher Mike Berry from The Sparta Florida Music Group over on the other side of the bar and had a bright idea. He went over and had a few beers off Mike. They had a chat and caught up, before Charlie came out with it: "Mike, I was wondering. The thing is, I need to borrow some money."

Mike replied along the lines of "I'm not sure, Charlie. Musicians are notorious for borrowing money."

But Charlie wouldn't give in: "I have an idea… How about you listen to this song. If you like it, I'll sign it over to you and you can buy me a case of beer."

At this point, the UK Subs had already appeared on Top Of The Pops, had had top 40 singles and a debut album on the way, which went on to reach number 22 in the UK album charts. Mike didn't really need to hear the song. It was a bit of a no brainer as far as he was concerned. So Charlie got his crate of beer and he returned to the party and they all got really pissed up.

Tomorrow's Girls came out a little later and went on to become a UK top 30 single, but Charlie had made a deal and he honoured it. He handed over the record.

Even now that single still earns money. It appears on punk compilation albums and elsewhere. I'm guessing it may have earned the best part of £100,000 over the years and Charlie handed it over for something like £20. Classic.

For Charlie, it was a gamble. Tomorrow's Girls might not have been a hit – and he wouldn't have had his beer!   **AG**

The little bugger

Andy Cowan-Martin was born with numerous physical problems, including suffering polio as a child, which left him small of stature, just 4'6" tall. He also went virtually blind later on in his life. His medical problems led him to spend a great deal of time in and out of hospitals, undergoing one operation or another. However, by sheer will and determination, he managed to overcome his disabilities and was successful in the music business.

I worked and lived with Andy at various times. We did several projects together including the Christmas Carol concert for The Royal Choral Society. He knew and was known in the business by virtually everyone – he was even a friend and admirer of Spike Milligan, with whom he had a similarly off the wall sense of humour.

Andy qualified as a dentist and I remember asking him why he gave it up. He said: "Dear boy, there weren't any vacancies for a blind dentist." He always sounded like a news broadcaster from the 1940s or 1950s. Not surprising really, as his father was high up in the BBC in Scotland during that period.

While Andy might be small of body, he was big in heart and guts. And boy could he get himself into trouble.

He was the manager of a small record company in Wardour Street in Soho, London. After a while working there, he got progressively more and more pissed off with the chairman. One day he told me he had had enough. He said: "Come with me. I'm pissed off. I'm going to have it out." So off we trotted up to the West End.

We arrived at the office, where an almighty row broke out. Andy started by calling the chairman an asshole, so the guy slapped Andy around the head. Simultaneously I slapped the chairman with my umbrella (bending it in the process) as I shouted at him 'You can't do that, he's only little!" Andy proceeded to punch him in the gut – how he found the target is a wonder – and the guy ran out of the office, screaming "Police! Police! I've been assaulted!"

It just so happened that a police officer was walking by on the other side of Wardour Street. She came across the see what all the commotion was about. "What seems to be the problem, sir?" she asked the chairman.

"I've been assaulted," he replied.

"Who assaulted you, sir?" she asked.

"He did," the chairman said, resembling an excited teenager, pointing at Andy.

The police officer looked Andy up and down for a second or two, then looked at the chairman. "I suggest you find someone your own size, sir," she said with more than a hint of disdain. She promptly about turned and walked off.

I grabbed Andy under his armpits and lifted him off as we beat a hasty retreat. **CM**

Bad Manners: wardrobe malfunction

I can't remember what town it was, but we were with Bad Manners on our way to play Bangor University. En route, we booked to stay the night at a gorgeous privately owned hotel, complete with inviting rooms and delightful furniture – a real home from home. The welcoming atmosphere was further compounded by the really delightful couple that owned the place. Very affable, nothing was too much trouble. They were very happy to keep the bar open 'til the early hours. Well, they would, wouldn't they? A 12-piece entourage eager to drink the place dry. Cynicism aside, their hospitality was really appreciated. We loved it, they loved it and we all had a great laugh that night.

Despite all the drinking, drugging, joking and pranking that have always have surrounded the band, Bad Manners never missed a breakfast. They weren't for lying in bed all day, but always wanted to venture out and soak up the locality, checking out attractions like old churches and markets and the like. The only problems used to occur when they enjoyed the sights too much and forgot to get back on the bus when they were supposed to. That was the norm, but not in this particular instance.

That morning, I stumped up to the owners. "Sorry I'm a bit late. Am I still alright for breakfast?"

"Yes, yes, yes, you're alright, the band are all in there," replied the owners.

True enough the band was all gathered down in the restaurant – nothing unsurprising there – and in I go. "Morning, morning, morning," I heard as I walked in.

What's going on? I wondered. The band were all being really nice, which was unusual, 'cos they were not nice!

Next thing, the band turned and said: "Um, we got to go, boss. We'll see you on the bus."

No problem, I thought, as they left me talking to the landlady and her husband while I finished having breakfast. I assumed they were going to have a wander around the town.

"They're lovely boys – ever so nice, no trouble," the landlady said.

"Aah well, you've been ever so nice yourself, really kind. It's been great The food is excellent, it's a lovely hotel and really well kept," I replied.

I was still chatting with them when Clint the tour manager came in: "We're ready to roll."

"Yeah, OK," I replied. I settled the bill, thanking our hosts profusely, before I hopped on the coach. On the tour bus, I used to like sitting in the dicky seat by the driver to start with, just having a word with him, while letting the rest of the touring party carry on with their noisy nonsense at the back.

That day though, it was very quiet behind me on the bus, which was not like Bad Manners. Not only that, they were all on the bus on time, which was also very out of character – you usually spent two hours looking for the fuckers.

The driver – John Watts his name was – was looking straight ahead. "What the fuck's going on?" said John, as was his way.

I had no idea.

"Right," I said. "We've got to get to Bangor."

"I know that guv, yep, yep," he said. "You wanna go now then… Uh, we should get a move on really."

"Like we've got plenty of time," I replied sarcastically. "Let's go."

We were just about to pull off when the the hotel landlady sprinted out, screaming like a banshee, husband in tow. "I want my furniture back!"

"I beg your pardon?" I replied.

One minute ago she was like giving me a kiss goodbye, now she was screaming at me.

The bus doors opened and I could hear this tittering behind me – and we're talking about a big fuck-off coach, so they were all right down the back.

The landlady sounded deranged: "They've stolen all my wardrobes!"

"Who has?"

"Your bloody band. They're thieves."

While she was spouting on, there was all this giggle, giggle, giggle going on in the background. I sat there denying the whole episode.

But she insisted: "They're on your bus."

"Oh, don't be so stupid. There's no furniture on the bus. Come and have a look."

I turned round and true enough, the whole aisle was full of fucking wardrobes.

But we needed to get going, so I just fronted it out.

I turned back round to face the front.

"Don't be silly, woman, there's no furniture here. You can see that for yourself."

However, by this point, the old man had gone and called the police. It was getting a bit serious, so in the end I decided to apologise.

"Yeah, OK, sorry," I said to the landlady.

I turned round to the band. "Look, you bastards, get it out of here. Get it back into the hotel."

There was the woman, her husband and a copper all standing at the front door as the band busily carried the wardrobes back into the hotel. They went in with furniture and came out emptyhanded. Wardrobes all in, band all out.

"Really sorry about this," I said to the hoteliers, trying to smooth things over. "I hope there's no damage done. Any damage, call me."

"Yes, well, probably better if you don't say here again," said this young copper in his broad local accent. "Or I'll have to arrest you."

We all got back on the bus and I yelled to the band: "You cunts!" Everyone was laughing like fuck as we finally got going.

We were about 40 miles up the road when I heard the nee-nah nee-nah sound of a police siren getting closer, followed by the screeching of brakes. It was another cop. He pointed frantically for us to stop, so we pulled over.

"Right, what have you done with them now then?" he said.

"Done with what?" I replied, stunned.

"The furniture you stole from the hotel."

"We gave it back. One of your officers was there – he saw the whole thing."

"No, no, no, no, no, you've run away with it."

I didn't even want to dare look back in the bus, but this time there was definitely nothing on it, there was nothing in the trunk. No problem.

At that precise moment, our fucking lighting truck went whizzing by and the guys on it beeped their horn and shouted out.

"Old bill, up yours," and all that kind of thing.

"Right, we'll have them," said the coppers. Off they went and a few hundred yards up the road they stopped the truck, opened it up and, sure enough, there inside was all the fucking furniture.

What they had done back at the hotel was simple. One of the band had been in collusion with the road crew and they had parked the lighting truck around the back of the hotel. As the band had taken the furniture back into the hotel, they just went straight on out through the back door and put it straight on the lighting truck!

We had to drive the furniture all the fucking way back to the hotel.

Eventually we arrived at the gig. We were a little bit late, but, remarkably, Bad Manners never ever missed a gig.

On arrival at the university, the promoter turned to me: "Where have you been? We didn't think you were coming."

"Oh, we had a little problem in the wardrobe department!"
ACM

Bad Manners: passport to success

Louis Cook was the guitar player in Bad Manners. He never had both oars in the water – lovely bloke, but he really wasn't with us.

He was with the band in New York at the end of a tour and we were due to be returning home to the UK the next night. We were sitting around the hotel bar and he came sauntering up to me and said: "I've lost my guitar."

"Oh right" I replied in a kind of resigned, here-we-go-again kind of fashion. For the record, this guitar was no ordinary instrument: it was a real class Fender Jaguar.

"Where did you leave it?"

"I left it in the hall outside my room."

"You left a Fender Jaguar in the hall of a New York hotel and now it's gone?" Like I said, Louis really wasn't with us.

"Yeah, what do you think I should do about it?"

"Bite the bullet mate, claim it on the show and you'll have to get another one."

"Right, OK."

So he was all miserable because he had lost the guitar he had all his life. I can totally understand that, but he did leave it outside his hotel room before he went to sleep – not a good idea. A bummer it may be, but we were leaving for home the next day and we could sort it all out later, world still turning.

Ah, but if only it were that simple.

Next day, we arrived at JFK. We got to the check-in desk. "Passports please, guys."

All of a sudden the magnitude of Louis' stolen guitar kicked in. His passport was in his guitar case and he can't get a boarding pass without a sodding passport.

At this point the rest of the road crew arrived. "Right, passports lads. You remember, you all had to keep hold of them for ID purposes." Normally, I would keep them all for safekeeping.

At this point, Kevin, the head roadie, pipes up: "Ah, I've got a bit of a problem, I got mugged last night and the fuckers took my passport."

Great. Now I've got two people without a passport.

"Anyone else not got a passport?"

At which point the bass player pipes up: "I haven't got one."

"You had it when we got here, 'cos I gave it to you when we landed in San Francisco," I snapped.

"Yeah, but I don't know where it is now though."

So now I had three guys in the band party with no passport.

Then I had a brainwave.

I got Fred Munn and Andy Gould, both British citizens from my management team in the US, and persuaded them to donate their passports to the cause. This was a real pain in the arse, but I did at least have an extra two passports.

We were still missing one numerically, but when you've got about 15 or so of us flying, you've got a nice big pile to hand in to the check-in clerk.

So the guy at the desk wanted to go through the whole pile. Spotting that we could be in trouble and simply wanting to get us all home, I gathered the troops together.

"Come here you lot. We're going to have to have to do a flim flam here, just for fucks sake do as you're told. I want you to cause trouble, right. I want you to piss this check-in guy right off, confuse him, but don't interrupt when I'm talking to him."

I got all the passports together and the tickets and we walked over to the counter. "I'm gonna have to check them," he said.

At which point, right on cue, the guys started causing chaos. "That's my passport" "That's mine, give it back" and on it went. After a while, the check-in guy was getting really harassed. One of the guys went round to the desk and started fiddling about. "These are great these machines. What does that button do? How about that one?" as he started pushing them all.

"Don't do that, sir. You just killed my screen."

"Oh, but what if we push that one. Would that help?"

At which point the bloke on the check-out lost it… completely lost it. He looked at me sternly: "Get your passports, get your assholes and get your asses out of this country."

He gave us a boarding pass each and we shot through.

We got on the plane. Take off, no problem.

Of course, when we to London I would have to get off the plane first to sort out the situation with UK immigration, to try and explain that the passports had got stolen or lost or whatever. On the flight over I was dreading that moment and couldn't settle, let alone sleep. Making it worse, we were on the red-eye, so would be landing at Heathrow early in the morning.

I scuttled off the plane first and bowled up to the duty officer. "I am quite prepared to surrender my own passport…" as I start sweating, thinking of how to contact our lawyers to confirm who we were.

"That shouldn't be a problem, sir," as he casually waved us all through.

"You bastards," I said to the band. "I've been worrying about this shit the whole flight."

All I heard in reply was tittering.

How times have changed. You'd never get away with that nowadays.
                                                                ACM

Buster Bloodvessel gets the arse

I asked Bad Manners singer Buster Bloodvessel directly for his permission to tell this story.

When the band first signed to CBS America, the A&R man from New York, a guy called Bob, and a load of other guys from the LA office turned up for the signing, while our agent Steve Barker also came over from London.

We always used to hook up with the 1970s rock band Uriah Heep. Boxy – Heep guitarist Michael Box – and the boys were with the agency as well, so we would follow each other around. We would go to their gigs and they would come to ours.

We ended up on this 60 day tour, a different city every night. We got to LA and the city is so big that we were actually based in the same hotel for four days to play four different shows, which was luxury. It was like being at home: you could actually unpack and settle in and you actually got to remember where the toilet was for once.

The hotel had an open-air atrium and in the middle of it was a huge swimming pool. All the bedrooms were built around the edge and the main bar of the hotel fronted onto Sunset Boulevard. Reception, coffee shops, bars, you name it, it was all there.

We finished a gig in Orange County and drove back to the hotel. All of the record company were there. Someone grabbed hold of me and we marched into a room where there were mountains of cocaine and guys sitting round chopping it up into lines.

Out of nowhere, Buster stomped in, bypassed the others and dived straight into the heap of white powder. The next thing we knew, we were all completely out of it and loads of the band and crew were in the pool and having a great time. My trunks were whipped off and thrown in the pool. All I remember is that everyone seemed to be swimming around like porpoises.

As we were larking around, lounging at the side of the pool was a permanent resident. She was a really beautiful black goddess. Buster spotted her, and really fancied her. What he didn't realise was that she was a hooker.

He was there next to her with the "Can I get you a drink?" line.

"No thank you, I'm not working tonight," she replied.

The penny dropped. "So you're a working girl are you?"

"Yeah, my night off. I live here you know."

He did a deal with her and whatever the price was, he was $50 short. So he came wobbling over to me, still there minus my underpants. "You've got to let me have $50."

"No, 'cos I'll never get it back," I told him.

He insisted he had to have her, so this debate went on for a while as it does when you're out of your head. Eventually I relented. "OK then, but you're going to have to work a forfeit for it," I teased.

"Yeah, whatever you want to do."

"Come with me then," I replied. We went through some glass doors towards the reception. I drew $50 out of the ATM, rolled the notes up like a cigarette, got down on all fours and shoved them up my bum. "You can have the $50 if you pluck them out with your teeth!"

Which, to my amazement, he did, before running off to his goddess.

Unknown to him, she had seen what had been happening.

"Right, I've got the money," he told her excitedly.

"Fuck off, fatty," she replied. "I've got more respect for my body."

So not only did I help to blow the deal, but what we also didn't realise was that there were 20 or so Japanese tourists checking into the hotel, who all saw this unfolding. Me on all fours, Buster in shorts (let me say, not a pretty sight) plucking dollars out of my arse. They all began shouting and commenting in Japanese, before hastily checking straight back out.

Once the laughing had subsided, the head of CBS A&R told me that he couldn't believe I was able to keep control of a band full of assholes, adding that it was admirable.

Control? My arse! **ACM**

Buster Bloodvessel short of options

We did the Isle of Wight scooter rally with Bad Manners. I don't know when it was – 1985 or 1986, something like that. The event was simply an excuse for 20,000 skinheads to muck about in the mud. There was torrential rain, it was disgusting and the whole place was like a quagmire.

The Bad Manners set was going down so well that lead singer Buster Bloodvessel got really, really carried away. He always wore shorts on stage, but this particular pair kept coming down, revealing his large builder's bum. As they started to slip down, the audience clapped and cheered. So with the adrenaline pumping, he decided to take his shorts right off on stage and threw them into the crowd. Great idea, until he remembered he hadn't got any spares!

Not only did he finish off the gig sans shorts, much to everyone's amusement, but there was a subsequent problem.

With Buster being the big fella he was – he weighed in at almost 31 stone for a while – it wasn't very easy to buy shorts that would fit him. We were not on Oxford Street. We were not even on the mainland.

Unsurprisingly, we had an unsuccessful search for a pair.

Undeterred, we got on the ferry back to Portsmouth with Buster in his absolutely disgusting, skid-stained underpants, his bollocks almost getting an airing.

We made it as far as the ferry's cafeteria before one of the passengers complained and, in a flash, one of the stewards rushed in and told Buster to get out. We ended up having to hide him in a cupboard so nobody could see him.

We arrived in Portsmouth. It was Bank Holiday Monday and we were due to play a gig in town that night. We spent the rest of the day looking for somewhere that sold shorts. We were in one shop and the assistant asked what size we wanted. We pointed to Buster, who had remained outside. "They're for him, but he can't come in."

"Why?" asked the assistant.

"Because he hasn't got any trousers on!"

Meanwhile, he was getting attention from the local kids. "Look at that fat man, mummy, with no trousers on."

"It's rude to point," we replied, as we tried not to piss ourselves laughing.

God knows how, but we did manage to sort him out eventually, just in time for the Pompey gig.   **ACM**

Bill Wyman framed by Spike Milligan

Understandably, the great majority of people were disgusted when the tabloid papers revealed that Rolling Stones bass player and rock legend Bill Wyman was dating a 13-year-old schoolgirl called Mandy Smith. Wyman had met her when she attended the BPI Awards with her older sister Nicola in 1984. Of course, the uncomfortable truth is that the music industry had known about the relationship for quite some time before the story broke in the press. Strangers and the press were kept out of the loop.

The relationship survived the scandal and later on they decided to get married. Despite the obvious age difference and Wyman's reputation as being a serial womaniser, Smith's mother Patsy supported the relationship. Of course the marriage didn't last long, but did anyone really think it would?

When they got married in June 1989, she was 18 and he was 52. The wedding was a civil ceremony at his Suffolk estate, Gedding Hall.

I was working at PWL, the label of Pete Waterman Entertainment, and we had put out Mandy Smith's album the year before. When the invites to the controversial event were sent out, I was lucky enough to be given one. I say lucky enough, because the wedding day turned out to be one of the best weddings I've ever been to.

Why?

Well, for a start, the Wyman and Smith families were both extremely weird. While it was well documented that Bill had started dating Mandy when she was 13, what was even more strange and less widely known was that Mandy's mum was also in a relationship with Bill's oldest son Stephen and they got married a few years later. So you had Bill, who was older than Mandy's mum, dating Mandy and you had her mum dating someone almost the same age as her daughter.

You begin to see the picture.

Nonsense prevailed that day. There was much hilarity and, of course, the champagne flowed freely. The world and his wife were in attendance it seemed, including the rest of the Rolling Stones and larger than life characters such as movie director Michael Winner, who took it in turns to go up on stage and make extremely funny speeches.

The real reason for that day being so memorable for me was the late, great Spike Milligan. He brought the house down. When all the speeches had finished, Milligan bowled in with this great round parcel. He walked right up to the top table. "This is for you, William," he said, handing the parcel to Wyman. "Why don't you open it now?"

Bill opened the package without hesitation… only to discover a zimmer frame inside.

Well, that was it – the whole place fell about laughing.   **ACM**

Kylie the soap star

I must admit it made me very proud to see all the successes and the accolades that have come Kylie Minogue's way. I wouldn't have predicted her career would have been so long or consistently successful back in the late 1980s. I remember her as a quiet teenager, naive to the music business and completely innocent.

I had the pleasure of working with her at the very beginning of her career. She came onto the music scene after starring in smash Australian soap opera Neighbours, of which she was the undoubted star at the time, one of the all-time great girls next door. Her character Charlene married the equally blonde and clean-cut TV heartthrob Jason Donovan. Their onscreen romance spilled over offscreen for a while and he also went on to enjoy pop success and an acting career, mostly in theatre.

When the time came for the pair to quit the Aussie soap, they caused heartache for millions of teenagers, but they would soon be bringing joy to that same army of fans as they started new lives as recording artists. They flew to London and signed to the hit factory that was Stock Aitken & Waterman (SAW), where I was the head of the in-house artist management company. If any of our artists already had a manager of their own, as Kylie did, I effectively managed the artist's manager as well, particularly if they were a stranger to the European markets and didn't know the right people to speak to.

SAW were at the height of their hit-making powers in the late 1980s and we were writing and producing hit after hit for artists such as Bananarama, Rick Astley, Mel & Kim and Samantha Fox.

Kylie's girl-next-door image and enormous fanbase from Neighbours made her breakthrough success with us all but inevitable. After The Locomotion and I Should Be So Lucky, the hits kept rolling with a duet with Jason Donovan called Especially For You, which reached number two in the UK chart and sold over a million copies. Hand On Your Heart followed in double-quick time. Innocent teenage bubblegum pop personified.

It wasn't just image with Kylie at the time. She was as innocent as she seemed at the outset, which surely resulted in her making one of the most ridiculous phone calls I have ever had the pleasure of receiving. I always chuckle when I think back to the day.

Kylie and her manager Gary Ashley, an executive at Aussie record label Mushroom Records with whom she had first signed, set off from London to do some promotional work in Europe, flying off to Madrid with no hitches. As was always the way with our artists, they were staying at one of the city's very best five-star hotels as a base while making TV and radio appearances.

One night, I was working late back in my SAW office in London. My PA poked her head around the door and informed me that Kylie was on the phone. "Put her through," I said. Ker-lunk click. "OK, hi Kylie."

"There's no soap in my room," she replied in her Aussie drawl, sounding traumatised, certainly traumatised enough to have forgotten basic phone etiquette.

"Yeah, right... so why are you ringing? What's the problem?" I asked, ever so slightly baffled by her trivial opening line.

"Well, that's the problem."

"So, you're ringing me up from Spain to tell me that there's no soap in your room?"

"Yes."

"Haven't you rung down to reception?"

"But we're in Spain and I don't speak Spanish."

"I know you are, but the hotel staff generally speak English in five star hotels, you know. I'm sure you can get this sorted out by yourself." I paused, another thought forming. "More importantly, why are YOU ringing me from your hotel phone in Spain. Why isn't Gary sorting this out?"

There was a slight pause. "Well, because Gary hasn't got any soap in his room either."

I quickly put down the phone without needing to hear any more. I could barely believe what I had just heard. I couldn't stop rolling around with laughter.

In the end, between the pair of them, I guess they managed to sort out their very own 'soap' drama.

A few years later, Kylie left SAW for dance label Deconstruction, still in her early twenties. She never looked back. She may have been an innocent teenager, but she certainly grew up to become the queen of disco and one of pop's true legends.   **ACM**

Sabrina at the double

Some of you may remember raven-haired Italian singer Sabrina, as much for her ample charms as for any musical prowess. She became famous due to her hit single Boys (Summertime Love) in the summer of 1988. It became a top five smash in the UK and sold something like 1.5 million copies around the world. The single also featured a provocative video, as all teenage boys and their fathers are sure to remember, which featured Sabrina bouncing around by a swimming pool in an ill-fitting white bikini.

Her pop career was curtailed for a while after she appeared nude in a men's magazine, but she still shifted 20 million records worldwide.

Around the release of Boys (Summertime Love), she had me running around London like a blue-arsed fly. Why? Because while she was staying in London, she decided to move hotels four times in three days without informing me – and I spent bloody hours looking for her.

Very early one morning I got in my car to go and pick her up from the Marriott in Swiss Cottage to take her to do the Radio One breakfast show with Simon Mayo. I got to the hotel and to my astonishment she had checked out. I approached the hotel duty manager. "Do you know where she went?"

"Sorry, sir," said the manager apologetically. "No idea."

"Great!" I then had to search for the equivalent of a needle in a haystack. It really annoyed me, as she knew our schedule was going to be very tight. Eventually I managed to track her down.

"I didn't like the hotel. It smells," she told me.

"Smells of what?"

"Not really sure," she replied, while continuing to insist she had to find somewhere else.

So we tried a Hilton in the West End. She didn't like that. Then we tried another hotel… she didn't like that either. At which point, I lost it and launched into a lecture, giving her my best hairdryer treatment: "Listen here, this is your first major hit record and you are over in London for the first time, so get on with it."

She had even been allowed to travel with a friend, a striking gay Danish lady. I forget her name, but we were paying for her too!

I continueD: "Do as you're fucking told or bugger off back to Italy and stay there. I'm not here to run around after you all morning. You are really annoying me!"

"Ah, but you are lovely really, darling," she replied, batting her eyelashes, her hypnotically gorgeous eyes piercing right into mine.

"Bollocks!" I exclaimed, trying not to get flustered by her charm.

I was not having it and told her in no uncertain terms to get on with the job.

We made it to Radio 1 by the skin of our teeth.

A few days later, on the last night on the trip, some of the guys from SAW asked her if I have been looking after her OK.

"Ah yes, he's such a darling. He's a grumpy fucker, but he loves me really!" she replied cheekily.

The next day, I managed to drop her off at Heathrow Airport, no problems. Rather relieved I must say, I returned to my office at SAW. I got through the door and, to my absolute horror, Sabrina was standing in my office, as proud as punch with a huge smile on her face… or rather, a life-sized cutout of her was standing there.

Some of the staff in the office had put 'her' behind my desk – nearly gave me a heart attack!   **ACM**

Angry Anderson hopping mad

There is a fair chance that many of you were mildly and inexplicably hooked on that smash-hit antipodean soap opera Neighbours. After all, some 20 million Brits were watching this bastion of adolescent naffness in the late 1980s and early 1990s. Once a day wasn't enough, either, for this show managed to be aired twice a day on weekdays – ten times a week! Quite what that says about the viewing public and, indeed, the BBC's budgets is anyone's guess. Thirty years later, it was still pulling in half-a-million viewers and lasted until 2022, when it was finally cancelled after nearly 9000 episodes.

At the height of Neighbours' popularity, Angry Anderson, the follically-challenged frontman of Aussie punk group Rose Tattoo, had a number three hit single in the UK with Suddenly, which caught the imagination of teenagers the length and breadth of the country. For this was this song that had played out in the background when sweethearts Kylie Minogue (playing girl-next-door Charlene Ramsey) and Jason Donovan (playing boy-next-door Scott Robinson) walked up the aisle amid cheesy flashbacks of oh so tender moments from their courtship.

Given Anderson's pedigree in Rose Tattoo and playing a villainous character called Ironbar in the film Mad Max Beyond Thunderdome, the soppy ballad Suddenly was definitely playing against type. When this song went nuts across Australia – only kept off the top spot by Kylie's own debut single, The Locomotion) – Angry Andersen, as one might expect, was touring the country and doing very nicely and a more bizarre mix you couldn't wish to see. Gary – his real name – was covered in tattoos, a real nutter, but a truly great guy. Here was this extremely rough diamond singing the song to the wedding of two of the holier-than-thou characters from a cleaner-than-non-bio TV shows. It was the very strangest of crossovers.

To give an idea of Gary's alarming appearance, Pete Waterman wouldn't even let him into the SAW building in London and I wasn't allowed to put Suddenly out on the PWL label, forced instead to licence it to Food For Thought Records (nope, me neither) just to get the song released in the UK.

By the time the single was in the UK Top Ten, we were driving across Australia in our tour bus when this fucking great red kangaroo came bounding across the road, happy as Larry…

BANG. The tour bus hit the kangaroo full on and it produced one hell of a thud.

We were all like: fuck, we'd better get out and see if it was alright. We got off the bus and the thing was sprawled out on the baking tarmac, dead as a dodo.

As you may expect – but not necessarily know unless you have encountered one up close – kangaroos bloody stink. Not to mention they are huge and weigh a tonne.

We puffed and panted and finally managing to lift it up off the road. We were all thinking this was a bit of a laugh, so we shifted this thing up into an upright position and got out our cameras. Angry took off his Rose Tattoos tour jacket and stuck it on the kangaroo, along with his pair of Ray-Ban sunglasses and we all started taking photos as we bearhugged it.

It was at this point the fucking thing came round. It wasn't dead after all, merely stunned. Well this thing upped and fucked off wearing the tour jacket and glasses!

The funniest thing was that Angry Andersen had left all his credit cards in one of the jacket pockets, so somewhere out there in the Outback was a kangaroo carrying an Amex card or two. You could just imagine it turning up at the next billabong, ordering a few beers and being able to put it on his card, sport!
ACM

Fatty Towers

Before his stint at Stock Aitken & Waterman, Andy Cowan-Martin had managed 1980s ska heroes Bad Manners, fronted by the rotund Buster Bloodvessel. Andy remained a mentor and confidante in Buster's post-Top 40 life, which included the occasional big gig or TV appearance breaking up the club tours that provided his bread and butter income and satisfied the faithful.

Carl Miller, Andy and I accompanied Buster for an appearance on the BBC music quiz show Never Mind The Buzzcocks. It had a regular spot involving a celebrity line-up in the style of a police identity parade, with a former pop star and four ringers, and the panellists had to guess who was the real deal. One of the panel, looking at the line-up of five large middle-aged men clad in identical dungarees, wouldn't initially pick a Buster: "I know which it is, I'm just enjoying the spectacle."

Backstage, in the depths of Broadcasting House in West London, Andy and I met Lauren Laverne, one of the panelists on the show as a member of up-and-coming indie band Kenickie, and with a major career as a DJ and presenter in her future. On camera, she looked petite and delicate, but in person she was tall and statuesque. By way of introduction to Andy, who she towered over, I told her that he had managed Kylie Minogue. Lauren lit up with girlish excitement. It was so charming to find this super cool indie rock vixen was an unironic Kylie fan.

Buster had a stunt double called Russell – with a bit more clarity and ambition, the two of them could have been quite effective social pranksters. As it was, Russell would shave off one eyebrow and they'd go into charity shops and freak out the elderly volunteers with surreal comments.

Buster had bought a derelict seaside hotel in the seaside town of Margate on the Kent coast and got a substantial amount of tabloid newspaper coverage with his promise that he was going to turn it into a destination hotel for the double-XL crowd, with extra big beds and gigantic portions served in the hotel restaurant. Of course it would be called Fatty Towers.

Carl, Andy and I made the trip to Margate to discover the reality, which was perhaps predictably wide of its promise. Sticky carpets, Christmas decorations still up in March, Russell (eyebrow still missing), a terrifying gang of bikers in the bar – and not a paying guest in sight. I had mercifully forgotten the following detail but in reminiscing for this chapter, Carl reminded me that the barman was called Spider because he had a spiderweb tattoo on his dick, which he would flop onto the bar on special occasions.

Margate itself was in pretty bad shape. Once a popular British seaside getaway, it had been in decline since the dawn of the jet age, with the few remaining functioning guesthouses populated by refugees from the break-up of the former Yugoslavia. The locals had seen better days too. I remember standing in line at the fish and chip shop next to an empty games arcade and overhearing a local man opine that he'd love to be Prince Charles because he'd love to bathe in champagne every day.

I hope Buster is doing well today. Through a random series of connections, he ended up contributing a wacky version of The Laughing Gnome – an early David Bowie novelty song from the 1960s – to a Bowie tribute album I compiled for Invisible

Hands Music, but our paths didn't cross. I do know he topped out at 31 stone, but shed the weight and enough of the persona to get down to a mere 13 stone. Hopefully his svelte new form will propel him to a ripe old age. Charity shop volunteers beware!

These days, with office workers able to work from home a few days a week and a 90-minute door-to-door commute bearable on the other days if it means being able to afford to own a home, Margate has come back up in the world. Ironically, a more polished version of an establishment as funny and eccentric as Fatty Towers would probably be quite a good fit in modern-day Margate.
CK

Irene Cara sings karaoke

The late American singer Irene Cara was best known for her song Flashdance (What A Feeling) and for playing Coco Hernandez in the 1980 movie Fame. She also recorded the Fame theme song. But to many of us in her road crew on a Japanese tour in the 1990s, she was known as a pain in the arse. Why? Well, let's start at the beginning.

I met up with Irene for dinner to discuss the forthcoming rehearsals and tour dates. To say I was not in the least bit knocked out by her attitude was a huge understatement. She didn't seem at all enthused by the forthcoming tour. One would have expected to get loads of questions – but absolutely nothing. She seemed more half-off than half-on about everything.

The first day of rehearsals came around. The band consisted of top professional session guys who had worked with the likes of Frank Sinatra. They all worked to a strict code of discipline. I'd told Irene that the band wanted a few hours on their own to routine the songs and could she come in at around 3pm.

By 5pm, the band were ship shape and Bristol fashion, but there was no Irene. She finally turned up at about 6pm. I could see the band were brassed off, but a one-off late showing is just about forgivable. However, the same thing happened every day for the rest of the rehearsal period, much to everyone's annoyance. This led to an unhappy ship and an under-rehearsed singer.

Irene was contracted to perform a 90-minute set and the band were also obliged to perform a 30-minute warm-up set of their own material, making for a two-hour show.

Unfortunately, Irene had under an hour of material ready to go. After some debate, the band agreed to play an extra ten minutes of their opening set, and with some between-song chitchat from Irene, we could just about scrape home. In hindsight, I should have seen this was an omen for what was to come.

Next stop Japan.

We all met at Heathrow as arranged. Naturally, Irene was the last to arrive.

I checked everyone in, handed out boarding passes and arranged to meet everyone in the bar airside after security and immigration.

Having sorted things out with the airlines regarding our connecting flight, I made my way to the bar to find the band having a preflight bracer or two.

"Where's Irene?" I asked.

"Last time we saw her she was round the shops," they replied.

OK, no problem. We duly boarded the plane. Irene was booked in first class while the rest of us were in steerage, so I didn't expect to see her until the baggage claim in Japan. After a good 20 or 30 minutes sitting in the plane waiting for pushback, I heard an announcement over the PA: "Can a member of the Irene Cara party please identify themselves to a member of the crew."

What the fuck is up now? The lead flight attendant told me that passenger Cara was not onboard. The airline crew were obviously pissed off because the plane couldn't take off with her bags onboard. "Could I please go and find her?" the crew asked.

So off I trotted, ventilating like mad. I looked around the departure lounge. No sign of her there. I spoke with immigration to ask them whether they would let me out to check the main hall. They did, but not graciously.

Anyone who has passed through the jungle at Heathrow Airport Terminal 3 can imagine how difficult it is trying to find someone there. After rushing around for another 30 minutes or so, I finally spotted her in McDonald's, eating a dessert. "Irene! What are you doing? We are all on the plane waiting for you. You're holding up the flight."

She gave me a vacant look as if to say 'What's all the fuss?'

Eventually we boarded to a chorus of hisses, nearly two hours late – and me feeling about two feet high. We didn't make up any of the lost time en route and landed in Tokyo too late for our connecting flight to Fukuoka on the south Island of Kyushu (as did every other passenger with a connection). After more blagging at the Japan Airlines ticket counter, I managed to get a connection three hours later and we finally arrived in Fukuoka, completely knackered after a 24-hour journey.

We were booked to play for a whole week at the Blue Note jazz club. I arranged sound checks and a run through for the first afternoon. About halfway through, I was doing something or other when I heard a commotion. Uptight voices were coming from stage.

I get on stage and asked them to calm it down. "What's going on?"

"He's not in time," Irene blasted at Geraint, the bass player.

I knew that was not on because Geraint was as solid as a rock.

Eventually calm was restored and we put it down to nerves. After the session, Geraint came over to me. "What's her fucking problem, I'm never out of time."

"I know mate, it's 'cos you've got red hair," I replied, trying to lighten the mood.

The atmosphere didn't improve. For the first two nights it was a huge stress to get Irene to the club and onto the stage on time. There always seemed to be a fuss over something and the band were getting really pissed off.

Eventually, I said to Irene that if she was not feeling great, she should see a doctor. I arranged an appointment and explained to him that she was stressed and asked whether he could prescribe something to help, which he did. After that, things really settled down and the week went quite well.

Then one night, during the walk back to the hotel after the show at about two in the morning, I pointed out to Geraint that a number of tents, all lit up magnificently, had sprung up. They hadn't been there during the day on our way to the club. Being curious, we peered in. It turned out that they were temporary canteens for the night workers, serving food and, best of all, they had huge urns of hot saki that they were selling for a couple of Yen a glass. The Japanese, being polite, invited us in and it became a regular pit stop for an hour or so every night after the show. We would stagger back to the hotel every night pissed as parrots. With a week-long run in the same venue, there was no travel or set-up required, so we could roll out of bed the next day at almost sunset if we wanted to and sleep off even the most monstrous of hangovers.

For the next leg of the tour we headed to the Blue Note in Tokyo. This club was bigger than the one in Fukuoka and we expected a decent highbrow audience. Unfortunately, Irene's mood seemed to have slipped back again. I guess the prescription had run out.

Her habitual lateness resumed and she seemed as morose as before. It is safe to say that there wasn't much bon ami between her and the band, who had been practically carrying the show.

On the second or third night in Tokyo, the band called a meeting and informed me they were going on strike. (You can guarantee that if a muso downs instruments it will be just before show time.) They pointed out that they were playing half the show and wanted more money. Of course, they had a point. So frantic calls were made between myself, the club and London to resolve the issue, not made easy due to the nine-hour time difference. We managed to reach a settlement and the shows went ahead as planned. However, the club was not at all happy and it left a sour note (no pun intended). It was not one of the best trips I've worked on, but it did have its moments.

We eventually got to the South Island. As we landed, Irene began to complain again that she was depressed because of her weight. She often complained she was overweight, that she wasn't at her dancing weight and so on. Someone suggested she take some tranquilisers. She did and she seemed OK for the next couple of days… until she and Geraint had another fight. This compounded what had been a far from ideal atmosphere throughout the trip.

At this point, I began to feel a little sorry for Irene. I realised she was having issues with her weight and also some other business problems. She was obviously suffering. Thankfully, she probably didn't notice the ill feeling towards her.

The mood in the camp brightened considerably towards the end of the trip, after a few of us suggested we all go out together and have a bit of a crack. We ended up in this bar and, as we walked in, some of the locals were performing Irene Cara tracks on the karaoke – the theme to Fame and all that. We went over to Irene and nudged her to get up and do one of her songs.

She didn't really want to, but she was a good sport about it and sure enough she went up and belted out one of her numbers. We all enjoyed the rest of the evening as other locals performed Irene tracks. Towards the end of the night, the judges voted for their winner.

They announced the winners in reverse order – fifth, fourth and so on. Eventually they announced the runner-up. It was Irene. She had come second in her own karaoke competition!

A local girl was judged to have been a better Irene Cara than Irene Cara. Well, you can imagine the laughs we had in the camp after that. If only we had stumbled on that karaoke earlier in the tour.

CM

Babylon Zoo get their kit off

I was the drum tech for a relatively unknown artist called Rob Reynolds one night up at the Borderline on Charing Cross Road in London. The drummer for Rob was a great guy called Darren Mooney, who went on to play for the likes of Primal Scream and Gary Numan. At the time, he was drumming for Babylon Zoo, who had a number one single in the UK called

Spaceman in 1996, due to it featuring in a TV commercial, and a subsequent album that crashed and died.

It was my first ever gig as a drum tech. During the gig, I got really pissed – two-dozen bottles of lager and a spliff or two, something like that. Nobody had told me not to drink during the gig at this point. I thought it was all rock 'n' roll the whole way.

"Completely strip the kit, Sam, completely strip it," I was told at the end of the night.

"What? Completely strip it?" I asked.

"Completely strip it."

So I did. Anything that would unscrew, unbolt or untie, I unscrewed, unbolted and untied. I put screws and nuts in one pile, skins in another, rims in one pile, clamps in one pile. Soon, the kit had been reduced to its components with such a thoroughness that it bore no resemblance to drums, just hardware everywhere!

As I was finishing up, Darren came out. He saw what I had done. The colour visibly drained from his face. I can only say he was speechless.

Not only that, but it was a rare kit, new on the market at the time. I found out later that he had to send it back to the manufacturer to get it reassembled and it took about three or four weeks to get it back.

What a start to my career! Thankfully, second chances did come around. **SC**

Primal Scream frontman honours The Kinks

I will never forget working on the revived Isle of Wight festival with legendary Kinks frontman Ray Davies in June 2005.

Now this was a really cool job because A) who I was working with, and B) the magical location. When I think of the Isle of Wight festival, I think of it as a kind of UK version of Woodstock, the event that kicked off at the height of flower power in 1968. There are many magical and colourful images that I see in my mind from that year and others.

The very first festival, held in the summer of 1968, had a modest line-up – if you call T. Rex and Arthur Brown modest. Another major image that is projected in my mind when you mention Isle of Wight is Bob Dylan in a stunning white suit playing to over 150,000 people in 1969. The most famous – or possibly infamous – Isle of Wight festival was in 1970, with Jimi Hendrix wearing his long sleeved kaftan-inspired psychedelic shirt, big hair and getting his groove on. The Doors, Miles Davis, The Who, Joni Mitchell, The Moody Blues and Sly & The Family Stone also performed, all at the peak of their powers and careers. It was filmed for cinema release as Message To Love and had 600,000 attending on an island with a local population of only 100,000. It was way out of hand. Thirty-two years passed before the next event of its kind.

It is Dylan and Hendrix that remain synonymous with the festival for me. They hover over it like some kind of spiritual and musical leaders.

Even if the festival is far smaller today than it was in the late 1960s, it remains a magical place – and there I was with arguably the major component part of The Kinks, another legendary London rock 'n' roll band of the 1960s. To me, The Kinks can be mentioned in the same breath as The Beatles, The Who or the Rolling Stones, they are one of the all-time great British bands and Ray Davies is the songwriting genius that drove them forward. And to think I was getting paid to work on this festival, with this great man!

The crew and I arrived in Southampton on the south coast of England a few days before the gig and hopped on a ferry for an hour or so to the island. We drove off and up to the site, lush and green and surrounded by woodland. We set up the show and it all went great. Although as I mentioned, the festival is smaller than it was in its heyday, there were still at least 50,000 fans at the Seaclose Park site, and The Who, David Bowie, REM and Travis all played great sets.

Ray took centre stage on a beautiful hot and sunny Saturday afternoon in blue shirt, grey suit and glasses, looking very slick and cool. In no time at all his experience shone through. He had a relaxed crowd up on their feet singing along as he played classic Kinks tracks like All Day And All Of The Night, Lola and the perfect song for that moment, Sunny Afternoon. It was a pleasure to witness a genius at work.

A couple of days later, I was driving back to London in my transit van, loaded with the equipment from the show, when I received a phone call from one of the crew asking me whether

I would mind going round to Primal Scream singer Bobby Gillespie's house, to remove a table, of all things. Having worked for the Primals on several occasions, Gillespie was familiar with me and vice versa, so I said there was no problem. The job was a little left field perhaps, but nonetheless a little earner as I wended my way back to my bed. I was absolutely shattered after partying down on the island, but the job shouldn't take long.

Several hours later, I pulled up at the front of Gillespie's Victorian house in Newington Green, a leafy village-feeling part of north London. I rang on the buzzer and strolled up the path to the front door, where I was met by Gillespie wearing jeans and a dark flared shirt. He welcomed me in and told me in his dulcet Glaswegian tones that he didn't want a particular polished chestnut dining table in the house and that he wanted it removing before his fashion stylist wife, Katy England, got back from a trip. On her return he would make up some story about the table having been taken away to be polished and then hope she forgot all about it.

We opened the back of my van to see how we were going to manoeuvre the table in for him, and, of course, there was a whole load of musical gear inside. He asked who I'd been working with. I tell him about Ray and the Isle of Wight. "Have you got one of Ray's guitars in the back of here?" he asked, eyes lighting up.

"Yes, I have– over there," pointing towards a couple of black guitar cases.

"Can I have a go?" he asked respectfully.

"Of course you can," I replied. How could I refuse?

Gillespie forgot all about the table in an instant. I could see the excitement on his face. We left the table outside the van and he clambered into the back to pick up one of the guitar cases and squatted down to open it. He had picked a turquoise and white lead guitar and started to tune it. My tiredness was pushed to one side. I realised I was about to witness one of those moments you wish you could record or stay in forever. I lit a cigarette and pulled on it hard, trying to savour the moment.

Gillespie didn't disappoint.

He entered his own little world. He must have sat in the van for 20 minutes or so, playing classic Kinks tunes such as Waterloo Sunset on one of Ray's guitars, singing along every now and then in Bobby's distinctive American-style Scottish tones. It was absolutely beautiful. I just sat there silently, in amazement at what was going on. I was at a private gig with an audience of one. And I was the one.

He finally finished and was absolutely thrilled. He carefully put the guitar back in the case, closed it and jumped out of the van. Get this: he even thanked me for letting him use Ray's guitar.

"No problem," I replied, trying to remain cool.

Gillespie trundled back indoors. Still slightly stunned, I lifted the table into the back of the van after my private show and headed for home. What a few days it had been. It certainly beat working for a living.

When I finally got to bed, I was a happy man. Not sure if Katy was though, when she discovered her dining table was missing!

SC

Missing tapes

One of Carl Miller's best friends was bass player Nigel Ross-Scott, whose posh-sounding name stood out again and again in the credits of records I had loved as a teenage music fan, including the number one album The Gift by Ultravox singer Midge Ure, the last Dexy's Midnight Runners recording (Because Of You, theme to TV sitcom Brush Strokes) and tech rock band Re-Flex, best known for their hit Politics Of Dancing.

Carl brought him to my office to meet me. Nigel was tall and charismatic and I was super nervous. He put me at ease immediately with a great trick that I have used countless times since. He sat down in the chair opposite my desk, gave me a big warm smile and asked "So, what are you up to?" People always love to talk about what they're doing, so it's an instant icebreaker and has served me well.

Nigel agreed to work with me on some tracks, initially as a personal favour, but our chemistry and shared musical instincts clicked and we started jamming and writing together, notably on a tune called My Spiritual Advisor, inspired by my friend Nerida Palmer in Sydney who was studying psychology.

Our first attempt to tackle the track, a seven-minute prog-disco workout, was at a great little residential studio called House In The Woods, but despite trying a couple of different drummers, it just wasn't shaping up to be what we thought it could be. Retooling and going for a harder, programmed style instead of a traditional band approach in a basement studio in rundown Hoxton Square in East London instead of bucolic rural Surrey paid spectacular dividends. Nigel and I played our cassettes of the finished mix non-stop for days after.

At some point it occurred to me that I didn't actually know where the master tapes were. I didn't need them until we had a few more tracks done to make up a record, but where were they? I looked everywhere in the office and at home and couldn't find them. Nor could I ask for help, because that would mean admitting I'd lost the masters for our miraculous moon landing of a track.

I was so desperate I decided to consult a hypnotist. I had tried to be hypnotised by friends without the slightest success, so I had my doubts, but couldn't think of anything else that didn't involve a humiliating confession to the gang.

The hypnotist lived a couple of streets away from Chessington World of Adventures, which was probably appropriate. I lay down on a fancy dentist's chair in her front room, which vibrated at high frequency to attune my waves, and she went to work.

I felt quite foolish and not in the least bit hypnotised, but was too embarrassed to admit it wasn't working, so I did my best to act as though I was in some kind of trance, which was quite difficult as she kept using the wrong terminology for the floppy discs that contained drum samples and synth elements that ran alongside the multitrack tape. She kept calling them "computer tapes", so in a voice that sounded like I thought a hypnotised person should sound (albeit with a vibrato, because I was strapped to a paint stirrer) I kept trying to correct her: "Th-th-they're c-c-a-ll-ll-ed fl-fl-o-pp-pp-y-y d-d-i-i-s-s-cs". At the end of the session I was still unable to remember where I last saw them. I duly paid the hypnotist and left in defeat.

When I got back to Epsom, I was greeted in the office by my co-worker James Dawson, who asked me if I had lost the masters and I begrudgingly admitted that I had. Bless him, he had overheard my phone call to book the appointment with the hypnotist, which had included a description of the missing items, and secretly phoned the engineers in the Hoxton Square studio, who had them all in their office awaiting collection. I hadn't called the studio myself because it never occurred to me that we had just left them behind at the end of the session (and probably because the studio was another entity I didn't want to confess to).

I was so grateful to be reunited with the tape and the floppy discs – or "computer tapes" if you prefer – and the track remains a favourite. It even made it onto vinyl in 2014, along with some other Aries Project recordings from the 1990s Epsom days on the album titled English Ghosts. I actually regret using that title because it would now be a great title for a more political bash about Brexit and the ghosts of empire, which England seems unable to exorcise.

Before I leave the topic of things lost and found, I must share a quick tale from around that time about a night out in London with Carl, Nigel, singer Rob Reynolds and Invisible Hands Music administrator Jon Shepherd. Nigel had found himself a well-paid role in film finance and was carrying a leather briefcase containing a laptop computer, which circa 1996 was probably worth thousands of pounds (and weighted a ton!). Indeed, it may have been the first laptop I'd ever seen up close.

We kicked off with a few drinks at the Royal George pub on Charing Cross Road, then moved on to see some bands at the 12 Bar in Tin Pan Alley and a few other spots. With a bit of time remaining before the last train back to Epsom, we stopped at the Royal George for a nightcap and, by chance, sat at the same table we had occupied many hours earlier. I've never seen so many different emotions cross a person's face at once when Nigel saw his briefcase under the table, left behind, completely forgotten, faithfully awaiting the return of its owner as we cruised around the West End. Some guys have all the luck!

CK

TV talent show star stuck in the bog

In 2005, I was working with an experimental UK band called International Love Corporation, fronted by a guy called Comfort, with Greg Bone on guitar. We were playing at a venue near London's Ladbroke Grove, a former working men's club where a lot of stars tended to hang out.

Anyway, we did the gig and afterwards we were at the bar and couldn't help but notice a large group of really good-looking girls hanging out with this young, handsome guy.

We couldn't quite place him.

A little later I needed to take a piss and went off for a 'refresher' while I was at it. I walked into the toilet and opened the door of one of the cubicles that wasn't engaged. Inside, to my surprise, was the handsome guy from earlier with a rolled-up £10 note in his hand, looking very surprised and sheepish when he saw me.

I finally recognised him. He was a major name that had come through one of those TV shows looking for new musical talent.

I joined him in the cubicle, locked the door and chopped out a line or two.

"Here, try this," I told him.

He didn't know me from Adam of course. Never mind. We were comrades for a few minutes.

I did a line of his coke and he did a line of mine. The next minute he couldn't seem to get it together at all. I offered to leave him in peace, pissing myself laughing as he struggled to get his act together. He must have managed to finally sort himself out as he went on to have a fantastic career.   **SC**

Good day to be a Trekkie

I have always been a huge fan of Star Trek, starting when I was a kid watching the original Kirk and Spock era of the series. I watched the animated series, I read the annuals, the comics, the novelisations. It had always been a very inclusive vision of utopia for me, the early show especially pushing many boundaries. Bearing in mind the show came out in 1966, it had Russian ensign, Pavel Chekov, a Japanese helmsman, Hikaru Sulu, and a black woman, communications officer Nyota Uhura. It showed the first interracial kiss on TV, between Captain Kirk and Uhura, and in the ultra-conservative climate at that time in the US, the only way they could get around censors or some viewers was by putting them both under some alien mind control, but nevertheless it was groundbreaking. Then, in 1987, Star Trek: The Next Generation came out on TV, and it became a weekly ritual for me that could not be missed. I remember going round to my friend Hugh's flat every Wednesday, we'd have a beer and a spliff and watch Captain Jean-Luc Picard and his crew explore the cosmos.

Fast-forward to 2003 and I was on the road promoting my single Sweet Mother. I'd been up and down the country doing shows and a lot of radio, and one of the appearances I was most looking forward to was on BBC Radio 4's long running arts and entertainment show Loose Ends, hosted by Ned Sherrin. I was booked as the musical guest for that week and me and Invisible Hands Music label boss Charles Kennedy went up to Broadcasting House to record the show.

We were met by the show's producers and introduced to Ned, who was very kind and quick to put us all at ease. I was given a piece of paper with the running order and timings on it. Looking down the list, I first noticed the name of author Will Self, who'd I'd always liked. Reading further, I saw the name Patrick Stewart.

"Oh my God, it's Captain Jean-Luc Picard," I thought.

By this time, Patrick had gone on to star as Professor Charles Xavier in the X-Men films. As a comic nerd who collected Marvel, this was crazy. I generally don't get starstruck but I felt seriously nervous.

Patrick came in and we all shook hands. I was powerless to resist the urge to tell him how much of a fan of his and Star

Trek I was, hopefully not looking like a crazy Trekkie, but he took it very graciously and we chatted for a while.

We were led into the studio and seated around the table, and I happened to be sitting opposite Patrick. I had a little soundcheck for my voice and guitar, then the show began. Ned was introducing us all and started to interview the guests. When it came to him interviewing Patrick, they started to play the Star Trek theme music. Unfortunately, they were playing the score from the original show which Patrick was not in, not the Next Generation theme. This error led to a magical moment. Patrick looked over to me and asked me: "Should I tell them or will you?" It was only a few words but for a moment I felt like I was part of his spacefaring crew, sharing an inside joke that only he and I were in on, just one of those tender moments of connection. I laughed knowingly and he was gracious in his interview segment.

Time for the musical part of the show. I started playing and, setting aside the fact that it was live and had four million listeners, which can always be a bit nervewracking, what was really going through my mind was that I was singing for Captain Picard. Very surreal.

The show concluded and we were all saying our goodbyes. I gave Patrick a copy of the single and we both walked towards the lift chatting. In the lift, I remembered the turbo lifts in Star Trek, with their distinctive 'thssssst' swoosh, and there I was standing with Captain Jean-Luc Picard of the starship Enterprise with a copy of my single in his hand, and as the doors closed I smiled as, in my head, I heard that familiar 'thssssst'.   **RR**

Usher disaster forgotten thanks to Beyonce

Carl Miller and I were in Puerto Rico in March 2005 with the massive multi-Grammy winning R&B star Usher. He was there to perform a one-off 90 minute show called One Night One Star: Usher Live at the 20,000-seat Coliseo de Puerto Rico in San Juan. It was to be broadcast live on US cable network Showtime, but it very nearly never happened.

Usher was quoted in the press as saying preparations for the gig were "rocky."

That's one way to put it.

The afternoon before the gig, we were in the final stages of setting up the show and everything was going smoothly. Perhaps too smoothly. None of us could have anticipated what was to come, that was for sure.

On the floor upstairs, above the auditorium, was a mall with shops and fast-food outlets and so on. It was here that the problem began and it was all to do with a hotdog cooker!

Unknown to anybody, the cooker was leaking gas. Unknown, of course, until it blew up. The whole upstairs area simply exploded. The place went berserk!

It was like the mall had been bombed, something out of a Bruce Willis or Arnold Schwarzenegger movie. The bomb squad was called in and they came stampeding onto the scene. For a while, people thought terrorists might have tried to blow the place up.

As far as we heard, nobody was seriously hurt, luckily, but for a while the whole area had to be evacuated as the building was investigated and made safe.

As you might expect, the explosion set off the sprinkler system in the building. As a result, hundreds and thousands of gallons of water were released upstairs. It didn't take long for that water to start finding its way down into the auditorium, dropping the 100 feet or so from above like some bizarre indoor waterfall.

This water would have been totally disastrous, as it would have landed on top of trailer-loads of electrical gear – but for one thing. Some of the crew had put loads of rolls of heavy plastic sheets over the kit the day before. We had all concerned that the equipment was going to get too hot during the show, so we effectively covered everything in a massive tent, and placed loads of fans inside so they would blow cool air all over the gear. If it wasn't for those plastic sheets, there probably wouldn't have been a show.

While all this was going on, rumours started to circulate among the crew that Beyonce was going to make a guest appearance on stage. The rumours proved correct, to the huge delight of the crew, and it felt like she distracted everyone from the stress caused by the exploding hotdog stand. If only she knew.

And I have to say that in all my time with artists, Usher has to be the hardest working of them all. **JM**

50 Cent:
body on the line

Thankfully, working as a tour manager or music executive means you don't often have to put your body on the line. It's not like we're soldiers bravely fighting for our country or anything, is it? The biggest dangers tended to come simply from the substances you abused your own body with. However, I do remember one particular day when I genuinely feared for my life – and no, it had nothing to do with me taking drugs or drinking.

The day in question arrived as I was working on a deal to sign up 50 Cent, the hardcore rap sensation and former gangster from New York's tough Queens neighbourhood, for a pay-per-view concert on Showtime.

Curtis Jackson – his real name – had actually lived the life most rappers only talked (or rapped) about. He was a big strong guy, tough and built like a heavyweight boxer, covered in tattoos. He had been sent death threats, stabbed and shot nine times while sitting in a friend's car in New Jersey in 2000. He had been to prison – six months in a shock incarceration boot camp, a military-style facility for young crack cocaine and heroin offenders. He had also worked as a hustler, selling drugs on the streets from the age of nine, taking over the beat from his mother after she was killed. Coming from that place and making it big certainly deserves a lot of respect. He was a prime example of the American Dream.

I wouldn't pretend to know him intimately, but from the times I met up with him, I found him to be a very smart man, very deliberate in what he said and what he did. He had a poise that some could perceive as arrogance, but I would have said he was aware of himself, his history and his achievements. He could also see the bigger picture, not just what was in front of him, but the whole lot. Working alongside him was an unforgettable experience. It allowed you firsthand confirmation that this man was the real deal. It also taught you that, without question, the hip-hop scene could be very dangerous.

No wonder Curtis was renowned for wearing a bulletproof vest. It was not a gimmick – he wore it because there was an ongoing threat of violence, which seemed to follow him around wherever he went. Around the guys, you could feel the tension. Everyone seemed permanently on edge, a little jumpy and suspicious.

When signing 50 Cent up to the pay-per-view show, I met with him late one afternoon in 2003 at the luxury Ritz-Carlton Hotel near New York's Central Park. Half of my time with him seemed to be taken up with getting past his huge entourage, despite me being a senior executive and obviously not a threat – a little out of shape, late middle-aged and with thinning hair. I arrived at the entrance for a meeting in one of the hotel boardrooms, where there was a procedure to follow and body checks to endure. Some of the XXXL crew, wearing football shirts and jewellery, carried out the searches. Just to get into the boardroom felt like an achievement. In total, around 20 or so massive bouncers provided the security. It really was a hardcore operation and the security felt much tighter than JFK airport. This was when I began to feel a sense of the whole hip-hop world. To be honest, it was really intimidating.

I was finally ushered into the gorgeous wood-panelled boardroom we had hired, complete with chandelier and 20ft polished teak table. 50 Cent and some of his management were waiting for us. Most of them were dressed in the archetypal hip-hop style – you know, jewellery, sneakers, baseball caps and massive fur coats. The contrast between the hotel style and the style of the crew was huge.

We had a good meeting that lasted an hour or so. All went smoothly. We talked about his show and what we wanted from the gig and what he wanted. We negotiated cash, terms and so on. We wrapped up and 50 Cent and his crew invited us to a gig he was playing later that evening as part of the Rock The Mic tour. The concert featured fellow East Coast rappers such as Jay-Z, Snoop Dogg and Busta Rhymes.

We accepted and piled out of the boardroom, through the luxurious hotel lobby, towards a convoy of black and white GMC limos with blacked out windows. We got in and sped off. We arrived a little later at the Jones Beach Theater, a 15,000-seat amphitheatre on Long Island. Jumping out, we were all handed backstage passes by theatre workers.

When everyone realised who I was, I was upgraded to onstage passes, meaning I could go on stage as part of the crew. Amused, a colleague and I accepted the passes.

A little while later we were all hanging out in the dressing room area backstage, when all of a sudden and out of nowhere, some of 50's crew started handing out lightweight black bulletproof jackets to all the guys who were going out on stage. I had never seen anything like it. This was serious shit.

It was a little surreal, but not to all these guys. None of them flinched, they simply put on the jackets and tightened themselves up. This was all done with minimal fuss and was clearly part of a well-established routine.

Ken and I didn't get offered any jackets – we were not part of their crew and there were no spares – despite the fact we were actually going out on the stage. I seriously thought about asking for one, but I kept quiet, as I didn't want to be embarrassed.

The rappers and crews made their way from the dressing room, us following at the rear. We came out on stage as lights blared and sounds wound up. What a buzz! We were rocking out in front of thousands of cheering fans, who were banked steeply in the amphitheatre, creating a wall of sound.

Ken and I were bouncing around in a very white, middle-aged way, when all of a sudden two things occurred to me. First, we were the only two white guys on stage, therefore we would be an easy target if anyone wanted to take a shot in the dark. Second, not only were we white (and dressed in light shirts), we were the only two guys on stage not wearing bulletproof vests.

I knew Ken and I were not part of the rap scene, but we were on this stage and I couldn't help but be a little nervous. Ken and I decided to hastily get off stage. We shuffled off towards the back of the set, behind the PA stack for the rest of the show.

The set went really well for the next hour or so, the crowd bounced and the sound was nice and tight. Towards the end, 50 Cent undressed to his white boxers. It was part of his bravado. Off went his trousers and, most daring of all, off came his bulletproof jacket.

I admired his bravery, because being up there on stage for just a few moments scared the shit out of me and I was not a target for anyone.

Over the following weeks, my friends and family laughed at me when they discovered the fears I had on stage. I even began to think how crazy I sounded for worrying about being shot. I knew I would not be a target, but what if a gunman had been a bad shot? What if a hitman wanted to send out a message by shooting one of the entourage? I may have been shot by mistake or got caught in the crossfire. If I had been shot, I would certainly have been the most unlikely character to have got caught up in rap violence to date.

However, when you think about rappers who have been murdered, such as Tupac Shakur and Biggie Smalls, I'm not sure I did overreact to being on the same stage as 50 Cent when you consider his and rap's history.

That job was the one time that I really put my body on the line for my work.   **JM**

Britney Spears has a bad hair day

There is always a major media feeding frenzy when stars as massive as Britney Spears do anything, no matter how trivial. When she was at the height of her fame, she could be taking out thee trash, going to the shops or simply going out for a drink or two, the press were always in pursuit. Celebrities like Spears, Madonna and Eminem have sold millions of newspapers and magazines simply by doing everyday things we all do. We just can't seem to get enough of this incredibly prosaic stuff when it's performed by anyone famous. As a result, hundreds of paparazzi follow celebrities around, waiting for the next 'newsworthy' moment.

I guess celebrities appear exotic and exciting to kids. It's true that fast cars, big money and bling are real perks, but when you have worked with these people for years, they just become your job and the fact they are famous becomes unimportant. Personally, I think working in close proximity to pop stars means you get to see the real them, not just the image they want fans to see. And the sheen quickly wears off with most of them. In fact, many rock and pop stars are nothing more than a pain in the arse to their crews, and it is true that they are not always the smartest of people, even if they are talented.

That said, I did sort of understand the fuss that was made in the press when Britney decided to shave off all of her hair in an LA hair salon in February 2007. I remembered the headlines: 'Is it the end for Britney?' 'Has she gone off the rails?' Not to mention the shocking image of her buzzcut all over newsstands for days and weeks on end.

In case you don't remember, the story went that she walked into Esther's Haircutting Studio in Tarzana in the San Fernando Valley and asked a stylist to cut all her hair off. When the hairdresser refused, Spears grabbed some clippers and shaved herself bald. She then drove to a tattoo parlour and had her naval pierced and two tattoos etched: a pair of bright red lips on her wrist and a black, white and pink cross on her stomach.

Whatever the reasons for her severe haircut that infamous day – divorce from Kevin Federline, two children in quick succession, dealing with fame since being a child, rehab, an apparently overbearing mother, unrelenting media pressure and removing evidence of drug use – it was not the first time I had known Britney Spears to have a bad hair day.

When I first read about her 2007 buzzcut, I immediately thought back to the time I witnessed another hair-raising experience with her firsthand.

I was working with Britney on part of her worldwide Onyx Hotel tour in 2004, which was due to include two shows in Miami. I was a senior executive for Showtime, the US cable channel that was televising one of the Miami gigs. At the time, she was promoting her In The Zone album while also playing smash hits such as Baby One More Time. You may remember images of her in a revealing PVC outfit and writhing around on a double bed onstage – those images were from that tour. The concerts went great and she was making a seriously large pot of money in merchandising and such like (in fact, I think she made over $30 million in the US alone, the highest sum for a solo female artist for a good few years). Unfortunately, the tour was stopped early after she injured her knee.

My stint came before her injury. I flew in to a very hot and sunny Miami from New York, a week or so before the gig in the city.

I never got too close to Britney, but found she behaved like a petulant little schoolgirl, almost like her character in the video of Baby One More Time. No matter.

Anyway, she was set to play live on March 28 at the glass-fronted American Airlines Arena, a 20,000-seat circular venue complete with palm trees on the perimeter and a waterside setting. The gig was going out live across the country on Showtime as a pay-per-view event and was also being sold to

TV channels around the world, including Channel 4 in the UK. The evening before the televised concert, she was due to play a practice show in the massive indoor arena to just a couple of hundred competition winners and their parents. That show was supposed to be recorded and filmed in case of any problems with the real show. We also took loads of promotional photos of her and used them in the build-up to the main event.

She knew the drill. What could go wrong, you may ask?

Well, the day before the promo gig, Britney had the day off. She hung out with some friends and headed out to one of the massive department stores in Tampa. Nothing wrong with that, except that, while in the store, she decided it would be fun to buy some hair dye. Not only that, she then thought it would be hilarious to dye her hair bright red! Next day, Britney showed up in Miami, complete with a mop of pillar-box red hair, just hours before the promotional gig.

Her manager – I think it was Larry Rudolph at the time – went absolutely crazy. He screamed that he wasn't going to let her record the programme because the colour of her hair didn't match up with the blonde hair extensions she was supposed to be wearing.

You can imagine the dramas that followed, the mood of the crew and the tension in the camp. Everyone was on a knife-edge, wondering whether Britney even wanted to help solve the problem. At this point, morale was low, tempers were short and laughs were thin on the ground. Nobody wanted to be seen to be having any fun.

Finally, a decision was made. Her favourite hairdresser – Oribe, stylist to the likes of J.Lo – was persuaded (for thousands of dollars) to fly in from New York without delay. He touched down at Miami Airport a few hours later and was raced over to the 'redhead' in a private limousine by some of her entourage. After a lot of nail-biting by the management, Oribe managed to sort out the mess. He re-dyed her hair back to blonde, just about matching it up to the colour of her extensions. The extensions were all subsequently put back in, just in the nick of time for her to record the promo show, fans blissfully unaware and the press having missed out on a story that would have filled their pages for days.

Sometimes stars really don't make it easy for themselves or for their management.

Britney was as guilty of going to extremes as anyone, but that's part of being young and certainly part of the music business. In her case, it has all been well documented.

Was Britney dyeing her hair the behaviour of a young girl having fun, the thoughtless act of a glamorous pop diva or a symptom of an inexperienced individual who was under massive pressure and beginning to crack? You decide.   **JM**

One for the crew

The story of rock 'n' roll cannot be truly told without the tales of the road crews and the characters that toiled endlessly backstage – without whom, the business would not exist as we know it. Artists have always needed someone to take care of all sorts of things, such as wardrobe, travel arrangements or even helping them find their way to the stage.

The modern breed of rock crew did not exist until the late 1960s or early 1970s, coming to the fore with the advent of rock groups who started to require sophisticated equipment such as amplifiers, PA systems and lighting rigs.

When I first started, facilities were non-existent. You slept in the van or in a railway station (popular as they were the only place you could get a cup of tea in the evening in those days). Things have come on a long way since then. Crews now enjoy sleeper coaches, hotels, organised catering at the gig and so on. There are also more females on crews now. Pre-1980s it was very much a guys' world, with few exceptions.

For me, one of the most enjoyable things about being a tour manager and putting together a tour was picking the crew. Getting the right individual crew member could be the difference between a happy and successful tour or a not so happy one. On a couple of occasions, I inherited some right bozos. I'm sure most tour managers would nod in agreement. It's a matter of getting a blend of skills, coupled with the right personalities, attitudes and team ethic.

Being a crew member is hard work mentally and physically, and comes with long hours to boot. You can be away from home for months on end. All hotel rooms start to look the same and the road is tough on relationships. There's no clocking on or off. You are there until the show is over, then you start all over again. The crew perceives the tour differently from the artist, probably better in some ways, and you certainly absorb more of the places you visit.

When I joined Cat Stevens in 1970, I was the one and only crew member, having to do all things wrapped up in one. That changed quickly as he rose up the ladder – so quickly that it seemed like a matter of days until I found myself elevated to tour manager, responsible for a full house of crew and band. My primary duty was planning and organisation, dealing with the band and, at times, being joined at the hip to Cat.

After my Cat Stevens days, my career path took off in different directions and I never worked directly on a crew again, although the kudos and experience of having been there kept me in good stead when it came to dealing with them. I like the idea of being one of the originals. I could always turn round and say: "I did that when you were in short pants." I always enjoyed their company and the banter. If you wanted a good night out, hang out with the crew. Even the guys in the band would admit to that.

This book is dedicated to the early pioneering guys who turned the role of tour manager into the profession it is today – a tribute to the many characters and unsung heroes I knew and worked with along the way. **CM**

Halcyon days

My record label Invisible Hands Music took shape in 1993 when I rented an office above an estate agent in Epsom, which was the town nearest to my parents' house to have record shops (Epsom Record Centre, Our Price) and a musical instrument shop (Bootleg Music). That said, even the tiny village of Claygate I grew up in had Sound and Vision, a small record shop that doubled as a VHS rental outlet. Every high street had a record shop back in the day. Younger readers will be amazed to learn that even Boots, Britain's national chain of pharmacies, stocked the Top 40 singles and at least a thousand LPs – everything in the charts, some movie soundtracks, some jazz and classical greatest hits and a chunk of deep catalogue.

Invisible Hands Music and the office in Epsom started out as a joint venture with my friend James Dawson, who played percussion in my band Night World and was well-connected with other musicians in the local scene. I had recently been to the United States after a minor success with a Night World track called Night Flight To Charlotte, and while in the eponymous city in North Carolina, I met Mitch Cooper, who led a psychedelic band called The Inn and ran his own indie label, Third Lock Records. Third Lock produced compilation CDs of local Charlotte bands, each of them making a financial contribution towards the production cost and The Inn got a track on for free. This arrangement appealed to bands because recordable CDs, known as CD-Rs, were not accessible until the late 1990s, at least a decade after the advent of regular CDs. The first CD-R burners cost $35,000 and were the size of a washing machine. In the early 1990s, paying to be on a factory-produced CD was the only way to get music onto the format, other than landing a record contract.

I copied the idea wholesale upon my return. A photographer from the Epsom & Ewell Herald came down to the office to take pictures of James and I with piles of demos and the cord of the telephone around our necks for a story. The local railway franchise that rattled carriages past our office operated under the Network Southeast brand and James came up with the name Fretwork Southeast for our album. For £150, each band got 50 copies of the CD and we mailed out 200 copies to record companies, venues, music publishers, journalists and the like, supplying the bands with the full list so they could follow up themselves.

By the time I was introduced to Carl Miller by the landlord of local pub The Rifleman, I was still very green but had a bit of momentum, with a CD out and a bit of an infrastructure. If we'd met any earlier I would have just been a plonker with a dream. Carl had been road manager and consigliere for Cat Stevens, one of the biggest acts of the 1970s, with some 1960s acts before that and a victory lap in the 1980s touring with the Kirov (now Mariinsky) Ballet and a stint at CBS (now Sony) Records. He lived in a semi-detached house in a side street practically opposite the office that had the cosy cottage feel, with a postage stamp garden between the back of the house and a steep embankment that held aloft the main Network Southeast railway line into London. I proceeded to spend the rest of the 1990s sitting at Carl's kitchen table soaking up tales of the road from the unceasing conveyor belt of characters that dropped in – members of Cat Stevens' band and Pentangle, singer Colin Blunstone and UK Subs' bass player Alvin Gibbs. Some of those tales have made it into this book.

The younger generation in the party house consisted of Carl's kids, Alex and Anya, plus Catherine Bransgrove, Tim Gebbett and Sam Card. I had a foot in both camps because, although

I was barely into my 20s, I was slightly keener on classic rock than hard techno and keen to soak up war stories from the older generation, so Alex, Anya, Catherine, Tim and Sam probably have memories of youthful debauchery that I missed out on because I was too busy at the kitchen table, lapping up tales of flying on the Pan Am helicopter into Manhattan with Cat Stevens or going to Woodstock with The Who.

Sam's arrival in the friendship group was a comedy of misunderstanding. He showed up at the door one day, a confusion of dreadlocks and hippie gear, asking for Alex, who was attending a very highly regarded Epsom private school that probably shouldn't be named for legal reasons. Carl asked Sam how he knew Alex, and Sam replied "I know him from [redacted] school." Carl assumed that meant he was a fellow student, but it turned out Sam wasn't attending the school, he was selling weed in the car park!

One thing that united every generation of the gang was the anticipation of a visit by Carl's dear friend Andy Cowan-Martin from Northern Ireland. My Aussie cousins and schoolfriends came in a steady flow to visit the United Kingdom and Europe, so I was very familiar with the excitement of an inbound relative or close friend from abroad, and fondly remember racing down the M23 to Gatwick with Carl to pick up Andy off the Jersey European Airways jet from Belfast.

Andy was the most unstoppable force I've ever encountered. Maybe four feet tall, steaming with righteous indignation, fearless in any confrontation, walking stick always at the ready to stab the air for emphasis or, on occasion, administer a good thrashing. He was such a music business institution that he could walk into any Soho pub (such as the Ship in Wardour Street, which remains remarkably unchanged even today) and there would be a sotto voce "Hi hoooo" in reference to the Seven Dwarfs, of whom Andy most closely resembled Grumpy. After arriving from Belfast on one of his visits, he tried to pay for postage in the Epsom post office with Northern Irish sterling, which the clerk did not recognise, thinking it was Irish pounds. Andy's patience quickly wore off, wondering out loud what the fighting had been about for the last 30 years. The exchange ended with Andy shouting: "Can someone buy this person a television!"

What kind of chapter would this be without some mention of hard drugs? We all used to smoke weed, but that's normal. In the suburbs, and with both limited budget and contacts, cocaine was something that happened almost never, at least in those days, but one such occasion immediately springs to mind. I was in the office with Catherine and a little dab of coke had come our way which we carefully, if inexpertly, chopped out into a couple of lines. Suddenly there were footsteps in the corridor, so I reached for a piece of paper and gently placed it on top of the freshly chopped rails, to avoid being busted if it the incoming person proved to be hostile and to avoid sharing it if it was an ally (one of many reasons to avoid cocaine: it makes you very selfish!). It was Carl, who read our guilty faces like a book: "Cocaine!" We could have been up to anything. Coke was such an outside chance, so rare in our circle, but Carl knew as only a career tour manager can know. It reminded me of an episode of The Simpsons in which Bart boasts that Homer can hear pudding.

Our Epsom scene fragmented at the turn of the 21st Century as Carl moved to the Midlands to tend his ailing mother, his kids went to university and other pursuits, and I put Invisible Hands Music temporarily on ice to go and work for music wholesaler Windsong International with Steve Mason and Dominic Plomer-Roberts.

I moved away from Epsom in 2003 to North London and restarted Invisible Hands Music with a fancy office in Camden Town, releasing records by Hazel O'Connor (best known for starring in the 1980 punk rock movie Breaking Glass), Rob Reynolds (couldn't stay away from a voice like that), 1990s indie power pop heroes Silver Sun, Stranglers lead singer and guitarist Hugh Cornwell, Japan bass player Mick Karn, electronic legends Tangerine Dream and many others. I toured the world with these acts, including several Glastonburys, Coachellas and SXSWs. My interest in the history of the biz learned at Carl's kitchen table meant I understood the importance of seeing a show at CBGBs in New York or having a drink at the Chateau Marmont in Los Angeles.

They were halcyon days and I'm always grateful for such an apprenticeship. The spirit of that era still burns bright inside. Can I take something from that previous century and carry it forward into the next? Let's find out. **CK**

www.ingramcontent.com/pod-product-compliance
Lightning Source LLC
Chambersburg PA
CBHW051805050726
47598CB00006B/2428